Egypt

and the Middle East

BY
PATRICK HOTLE, Ph.D.

COPYRIGHT © 1995 Mark Twain Media, Inc.

ISBN 1-58037-052-7

Printing No. CD–1839

Mark Twain Media, Inc., Publishers
Distributed by Carson-Dellosa Publishing Company, Inc.

TABLE OF CONTENTS

INTRODUCTION

In the mid-1980s, I took a job teaching history at the Cairo-American College. I brought many prejudices with me when I landed in Egypt. As a child growing up in the sixties, my perception of the Middle East had been shaped by television images of Arab terrorists and short, sharp wars. Even today, the selective nature of television continues to emphasize violence in the Middle East. What I found in Egypt was far different. Instead of fanatical terrorists, I found the Egyptians to be incredibly generous, tolerant, and kind. They took their religion very seriously, but as a result I always felt safe and secure wherever I went. Their faces also revealed a wise patience born of a culture that had watched civilizations, including their own, rise and fall for at least five thousand years. American civilization, too, would pass like all the rest. We have much to learn from a part of the world that has seen so many years and so many approaches to life. This book seems a terribly brief attempt to cover so huge a subject. All that I can do is brush away a little sand and begin to trace the mysterious shapes revealed underneath. It is up to the reader to dig deeper on his or her own.

—THE AUTHOR—

Time Line for the Middle East

In the western world we usually record years by reference to a year thought to be that of the birth of Jesus Christ or the year 1. The years before that are noted by how many years before that date they occurred and are written with the abbreviation B.C. after them. Therefore, 500 B.C. came before 200 B.C. After the birth of Christ, we use the abbreviation A.D., which means *Anno Domine,* the Latin phrase for "the year of our Lord." However, instead of counting the years backwards, as we do for B.C., we count the years forwards up to the present year. In the very ancient past, it is impossible to know exact dates, so ca. is written before the date as an abbreviation of the Latin word *circa,* which means "around" or "about."

Before 10,000 B.C.	Neolithic Revolution begins.
ca. 9500 B.C.	Jericho occupied.
ca. 3500–3000 B.C.	The development of civilization in Sumer.
ca. 3000 B.C.	Invention of writing in Mesopotamia.
ca. 3000 B.C.	Narmer unites Egypt.
ca. 2686–2160 B.C.	The Egyptian Old Kingdom.
ca. 2600 B.C.	The Pyramid of Khufu is constructed.
ca. 2500 B.C.	Lugals or kings appear in Mesopotamia.
ca. 2334–2279 B.C.	Sargon is king of Akkad.
ca. 2040 B.C.	Nebhepetre Mentuhotep reunifies Egypt.
ca. 2040–1633 B.C.	The Egyptian Middle Kingdom.
ca. 2000 B.C.	The Epic of Gilgamesh is written.
ca. 1800–1600 B.C.	Phoenicians develop alphabet.
ca. 1800 B.C.	Hyksos invasion of Egypt begins.
ca. 1800 B.C.	Abraham leads people out of Ur.
ca. 1792–1750 B.C.	Hammurabi is king of Babylonia.
ca. 1558–1085 B.C.	The Egyptian New Kingdom.
ca. 1558–1533 B.C.	Pharaoh Amosis I drives out the Hyksos.
ca. 1512–1500 B.C.	Thutmose I rules Egypt.
ca. 1490–1469 B.C.	Queen Hatshepsut rules Egypt.
ca. 1490–1436 B.C.	Thutmose III rules Egypt.
ca. 1450–1200 B.C.	Hittite empire thrives.
ca. 1364–1347 B.C.	Amenhotep IV (Akhenaton) rules Egypt, also known as the Amarna period.
ca. 1347–1337 B.C.	Tutankhamen rules Egypt.
ca. 1300 B.C.	Moses leads Hebrews out of Egypt.

ca. 1300–1287 B.C.	Pharaoh Seti I wins back lost lands.
ca. 1286 B.C.	The battle of Kadesh.
ca. 1270–1220 B.C.	Ramses II, ruler of Egypt, builds Karnak.
ca. 1198–1166 B.C.	Pharaoh Ramses III resists invasion of Sea Peoples.
ca. 1000–961 B.C.	David is king of Israel.
ca. 961–922 B.C.	Solomon oversees golden age of Israel.
ca. 922 B.C.	Judah breaks off from Israel.
ca. 722 B.C.	Assyrians destroy Israel.
ca. 700–500 B.C.	Assyrian empire thrives.
ca. 586 B.C.	Chaldeans destroy Jerusalem and begin the Babylonian captivity.
ca. 571 B.C.	Phoenician city of Tyre falls to Chaldeans.
ca. 550 B.C.	Cyrus the great establishes the Persian Empire.
ca. 550–350 B.C.	Persian Empire thrives.
460–430 B.C.	The golden age of Athens.
338 B.C.	Philip of Macedon defeats Athens.
336–323 B.C.	Reign of Alexander the Great.
264 B.C.	Rome controls all of Italy.
31 B.C.	Battle of Actium.
ca. 4 B.C.	Jesus Christ born.
29 B.C. to A.D. 14	Most of the Middle East falls under Roman control.
A.D. 10–200	Pax Romana.
A.D. 70	Jerusalem destroyed by Titus and beginning of the Diaspora.
A.D. 284–305	Diocletian is emperor of Rome and empire is divided.
312	Emperor Constantine issues Edict of Milan, granting toleration to Christians.
330	Constantinople is constructed and beginning of Byzantine civilization.
610	Mohammed called upon to begin Islam.
632	Islam begins to spread to Middle East.
640	Persia comes under Moslem rule.
711	Moslem invasion of Spain.
738	Arab merchant colony in Canton, China.
762	Abbasid Caliph al-Mansur moves capital to Baghdad.
813	The mathematician Chwarazmi thrives in Baghdad; coins the term *algebra*.
925	The Arab physician Rhases dies.
1055	Seljuk Turks seize Baghdad.

1099	First Crusade captures Jerusalem.
1154	Mohammed al-Idrisi finishes circular map of the world.
1187	Saladin recaptures Jerusalem from crusaders.
1204	Fourth Crusade captures Constantinople from Byzantine emperor.
1258	Mongols capture Baghdad and end the Caliphate.
1353	Alhambra completed in Granada, Spain.
1453	Constantinople falls to the Ottomans and ends the Roman Empire in the East.
1492	Last Moslem stronghold in Spain (Granada) falls to Ferdinand and Isabella.
1498	Portuguese explorer Vasco de Gama sails to India via the Cape of Good Hope.
1520	Suleiman the Magnificent begins his 46-year reign.
1529	Ottoman siege of Vienna fails.
1699	Ottoman Empire begins to lose territory in Europe.
1774	Ottomans lose territory to the Russians at the treaty of Kuchuk Kainarji.
1798	Napoleon invades Egypt.
1805	Mohammed Ali becomes ruler of Egypt.
1828	First Arab language newspaper established in Egypt.
1829	Greece wins independence from Ottomans.
1839	The Tanzimat era of reform begins in the Ottoman Empire.
1854–1856	Crimean War.
1869	Suez Canal opened.
1897	First Zionist congress in Basel, Switzerland.
1898	Ottomans persuaded to extend railroad to Baghdad by German Kaiser.
1907	Britain and France agree to divide domination of Persia between them.
1908	Young Turks seize control of the Ottoman Empire.
1914	Assassination of Archduke Franz Ferdinand begins World War I.
1915	Gallipoli landing fails to capture Dardanelles; Lawrence of Arabia operating against Turks.
1917	United States enters the war. Wilson announces Fourteen Points. The British cabinet approves the Balfour Declaration.
1918	Ottoman Empire surrenders. World War I ends.
1918–1920	Mandate system established.
1922	Ataturk deposes last Ottoman sultan; proclaims Turkey a republic.

1925	French crush rebellion in Damascus and Reza Khan comes to power in Iran.
1930	Syria writes a constitution but remains under French control.
1931	Iraq granted independence.
1936	British troops leave Cairo but occupy the Suez Canal; Palestinian Arab riots.
1937	Peel Commission sent to Palestine.
1939	World War II begins; British White Paper denies policy of creating Jewish state.
1941	Lebanon granted independence. Rashid Ali becomes premier of Iraq; Mohammed Riza Pahlavi becomes shah of Iran.
1942	Battle of El Alamein.
1945	Syria granted independence.
1946	Transjordan granted independence.
1948	Jewish state of Israel created; war between Israel and Arab States.
1949	Ben-Gurion becomes prime minister of Israel.
1951	Iranian Premier Mossadegh nationalizes Anglo-Iranian Oil Company.
1953	Hussein becomes king of Jordan; U.S.–aided coup overthrows Mossadegh.
1954	Nasser comes to power in Egypt.
1956	Suez Canal Crisis.
1958	United Arab Republic formed; Iraqi coup kills king.
1960	OPEC formed.
1961	Kuwait granted independence.
1964	Ayatollah Khomeini exiled from Iran; foundation of Palestine Liberation Organization (PLO).
1967	Six day war.
1968	Charter of the PLO drafted.
1969	PLO chooses Arafat as leader.
1970	PLO expelled from Jordan.
1973	Yom Kippur War; OPEC raises price of oil 400 percent.
1977	Kuwait nationalizes oil wells; Egyptian President Anwar Sadat visits Israel.
1978	U.S.–brokered peace between Israel and Egypt. Shah Mohammed Riza Pahlavi imposes martial rule in Iran.

1979	Egypt expelled from Arab League. Radical Moslems seize Grand Mosque in Mecca; failed coup attempt in Saudi Arabia; Iranian revolution, led by Khomeini, expels Shah; U.S. hostages taken; Saddam Hussein becomes President of Iraq; Egyptian-Israeli treaty signed by Sadat and Israel's Prime Minister, Menachem Begin, at Camp David.
1980	Iran-Iraq war begins; U.S. attempt to free hostages in Iran fails.
1981	U.S. hostages held by Iranian militants are released.
1985	Egypt re-admitted to Arab League.
1987	Intifada begins and Iraqi missiles hit U.S. destroyer.
1988	Iran-Iraq War ends.
1990	Iraq invades Kuwait.
1991	Operation Desert Shield/Desert Storm launched against Iraq.
1992	Madrid Peace Conference creates plan for Palestinian self-rule.

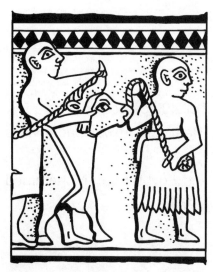

LANDING IN THE MIDDLE EAST

You awake to find yourself 10,000 feet above the deep blue of the Mediterranean Sea. Your last memory before dozing off was of landing in Paris's Charles de Gaulle Airport for refueling before continuing your journey. As you stretch your legs, you notice a crescent-shaped moon that has not yet faded in the morning light. When you look down again, you see the coast of a huge, reddish-brown land mass striped with lines of green in the shape of a fan. Here the Nile Delta flows into the sea. Your plane banks as it prepares to land and you gaze down upon a densely constructed city of narrow streets and high, thin towers the color of sand. This is Cairo, Egypt, and you have arrived in the Middle East.

The term *Middle East* refers to an area of the world made up of the present-day countries of Egypt, Syria, Jordan, Lebanon, Israel, Iran,

Cairo, Egypt, is located on the Nile at the point where the river starts to fan out into its delta.

Iraq, Saudi Arabia, Kuwait, Bahrain, Qatar, the United Arab Emirates, Oman, South Yemen, Yemen, Sudan, and Turkey. The term is also used to describe the culture of other nations that border those listed above, such as Libya, Algeria, Morocco, Afghanistan, Turkistan, and Pakistan. Even though people in the Middle East call their area of the world by that name, the term itself originated in the United States just before World War I. Therefore, it is a very modern term and reflects a view of the world from Washington or New York. The Middle East, however, is a very ancient place, and for much of its history, it saw itself, very reasonably, as the center of the world. Europe and later the Americas were only on the periphery. Later it was seen as merely a bridge or crossroads to be fought over by outsiders, but in more recent times, the Middle East has again become the center of the world's attention.

The geographical features of the area have been important throughout its history. First, its location as a bridge between Africa, Europe, and Asia has meant that a constant flow of peoples, tribes, armies, merchants, and pilgrims have entered the Middle East. Much of the land is made up of flat, arid grasslands or desert, so it was easy for invaders to enter the area. Yet, there are also rugged mountainous regions for groups of people to go to in order to maintain their independence. Many of the invaders stayed to enjoy the advanced civilization and the wealth of the area, while others spread what they had seen and heard in the Middle East throughout the three continents. The Middle East is also a bridge between the Mediterranean Sea and the Red Sea, which opens into the Indian Ocean. Thus, it became important to trade between Europe and Asia. This became especially true after the Suez Canal was cut through the narrow isthmus dividing the Mediterranean and the Red Sea.

Secondly, the Middle East encompasses a large area. Even if North Africa, Afghanistan, Pakistan, and Turkistan are excluded, the land mass of the Middle East is still the same size as the continental United States.

Finally, the Middle East is hot and dry. In some parts daytime temperatures shoot up past 120 degrees Fahrenheit. Much of it is barren desert. Because of the sparse rainfall, agriculture has always been dependent upon almost constant irrigation. In fact, the aridity of the Middle East played a crucial role in the emergence of civilization. Much of human history was made in an arc of territory that runs from the Nile Valley, up along the eastern coast of the Mediterranean, around the northern edge of the Syrian Desert, and down the Euphrates River Valley. This area is called the Fertile Crescent. Fertile it may be, but because of the aridity in most of the crescent, the rich soil would only produce with the help of river irrigation. This meant that early human settlement occurred along the two main river systems in the Middle East—the Nile in Egypt and the Tigris and Euphrates in modern-day Iraq.

As the early inhabitants of this area came up with answers to the problems presented by irrigation, they also discovered technology and ways of organizing themselves that had not been thought of by anyone anywhere before. The result of their activity was the dawning of civilization.

Discussion

1. Why did civilization first appear in the Fertile Crescent?
2. How does the term *Middle East* demonstrate the domination of Europe and America?
3. How was civilization spread from the Middle East?
4. How has geography been important in the history of the Middle East?

Map Activity

Using map A, locate and label the countries of Egypt, Syria, Jordan, Lebanon, Israel, Iran, Iraq, Saudi Arabia, Kuwait, Bahrain, Qatar, the United Arab Emirates, Oman, South Yemen, Yemen, Sudan, and Turkey. Also label the Mediterranean, the Aegean Sea, the Black Sea, the Indian Ocean, the Arabian Sea, and the Red Sea. Then label the Persian Gulf, the Nile River, and the Tigris and Euphrates Rivers. Shade in the arc of the Fertile Crescent. Draw in and label the Suez Canal.

Name _____ Date _____

CHALLENGES

1. Describe the view of the Nile delta from above.

_____

_____

2. What countries make up the modern Middle East?

_____

_____

3. What countries share the culture of the Middle East but only border on it?

_____

4. Where did the term *Middle East* come from?

_____

_____

5. The fact that the Middle East is a land bridge between continents had what impact on the area?

_____

_____

6. How large is the Middle East?

_____

7. Because the Middle East is arid, what is agriculture dependent on?

_____

8. How did irrigation lead to civilization?

_____

_____

9. Upon what rivers did settlement occur in the Middle East?

_____

10. Describe the area included by the name "Fertile Crescent."

_____

_____

BONES FROM THE DISTANT PAST: THE NEOLITHIC REVOLUTION

The archaeologist took out his small brush and carefully removed the remaining dirt from the fragment of human skull. To help him reconstruct the life of the long-dead human, he could look at the other artifacts found in the grave. There were broken pieces of roughly-formed, earth-colored pottery, a stone pick-ax for tilling the soil, sheep bones, and tiny clay beads. Based on the evidence, it seemed likely that this human must have lived during the Neolithic Age.

Scholars still debate over the origins of human society, but most agree that sometime before 10,000 B.C. the Neolithic Revolution occurred. Neolithic means "new

Archaeologists call the period when early man began to settle in agricultural villages the Neolithic Revolution.

stone age." This refers to a change in the way of life of early man from mobile hunting and gathering to settled agriculture in villages. An important part of the explanation for this change has to do with the climate. The earth became warmer around this time, and new kinds of animal and plant life flourished. Humans learned that they could be assured of food by planting wild wheat and wild barley. They also learned to domesticate animals like dogs, sheep, and horses. The wild wheat and barley were so easy to harvest that there was no reason to move on in search of food. People began to live permanently in settled villages. It is hard to know how early Neolithic farmers divided the labor, but archaeologists believe that women played a crucial role in the discovery and development of agriculture.

Life became even easier with new inventions like pottery, which was discovered in Iran around 6500 B.C. Others invented weaving in what is now modern-day Turkey. Still others nearby began to use crude carts on wheels to haul food. Now Neolithic humans could store food from year to year and build up surpluses.

With extra supplies some people could also specialize in certain skills, like making pottery or beads or tools. Earlier discoveries could be refined. For example, potters began to decorate their work with beautiful designs. They also experimented with new shapes and materials. The discovery of the potter's wheel enabled the potter to make jugs, dishes, and containers much more easily. Where before a pot would take days to make, now it took only minutes.

Others specialized in knowledge of the climate and the changing seasons so important to farming communities. Because these things seemed mysterious to the rest of the community, these men in time were respected as magicians or priests. At the same time,

           4

certain farmers expanded their holdings and gained power over others. Because of these changes, new social and economic classes emerged. With these advances also came new needs and further outlets for human creativity. As society became more complex, there was a greater need to record and pass on information. Thus, writing was invented, and with it came civilization.

At first Neolithic humans lived in caves or huts made of mud, reeds, or logs. These early dwellings were grouped in small, open villages. The purpose of the village was to form a community of workers who could share the jobs of planting, sowing, and harvesting crops and caring for livestock. The Neolithic age was a dangerous time to live, however. Predatory animals and humans might attack the herds or steal the precious food supplies. Therefore, farmers formed larger communities where they could help to protect each other and their livelihoods. Remains of Neolithic villages have been found all over Europe, Africa, and Asia. However, the most extensive remains of Neolithic villages and towns appear in the Middle East.

One of the best-known of these sites is the Neolithic town of Jericho in Palestine near the Dead Sea. The town dates back to at least 9500 B.C. The inhabitants built massive walls for protection against invaders or floods. They also constructed a great tower 28 feet tall and 33 feet in diameter. To accomplish such a feat, the inhabitants must have been well organized and disciplined. They also built structures for religious practice. Here, statuettes of an Earth Mother have been found. The inhabitants worshipped her in the hope that she would make the land fertile for agriculture. Archaeologists estimate that around 2,000 people lived within the enclosed 13-acre town. There, they cultivated barley and wheat, domesticated goats, and traded salt for obsidian and turquoise.

It is important to remember, however, that development and change occurred at a very slow pace. At least 5,000 years separated the beginning of the Neolithic Revolution from the first civilization. The next important stage of human development occurred elsewhere in the Middle East, in a land between two rivers that the Greeks called Mesopotamia.

Discussion

1. How did the Neolithic Revolution cause the emergence of social and economic classes?
2. What conclusions can you draw about the people who lived in Jericho from the remnants of their city?
3. What caused the Neolithic Revolution?
4. Based on the other artifacts, why would the archaeologist in the opening paragraph believe he was looking at the skull of a Neolithic human?

Map Activity

Using map B, locate and label the Mediterranean Sea, the Dead Sea, the Jordan River, the Sea of Galilee, and the modern cities of Jerusalem, Beirut, and Damascus. Label the modern states of Israel, Jordan, Lebanon, and Syria. Finally, using a pen or pencil of a different color, locate ancient Jericho on the northern tip of the Dead Sea.

Name _____ Date _____

CHALLENGES

1. What does Neolithic mean?

_____

2. When do archaeologists believe the Neolithic Revolution occurred?

_____

3. What was the Neolithic Revolution?

_____

_____

4. What did Neolithic humans learn to plant so that they would be assured of food?

_____

5. How did pottery make life easier for Neolithic humans?

_____

_____

6. What accompanied the ability to write?

_____

7. What is the name of the best-known Neolithic site?

_____

8. Where did the Neolithic Revolution occur?

_____

9. Why do we believe that the residents of Jericho were well organized and disciplined?

_____

_____

10. Do we know why the inhabitants of Jericho built walls?

_____

_____

_____

THE DAWN OF CIVILIZATION

What is civilization? It is not easy to define, but archaeologists look for certain characteristics that, if present, suggest a civilized society. First, they look for evidence of a hierarchy. In a hierarchy different social classes possess different privileges. Those in the wealthier and smaller social classes have more power than the more numerous but poorer classes "below" them. In fact, the upper classes usually rule over the lower classes.

Other characteristics of civilization include formal political and religious institutions, monumental architecture, and finally, writing. The first civilization that we know of emerged between 3500 and 3000 B.C. in Mesopotamia. This is the name for the Tigris-Euphrates River Valley of mod-

Donations of grain brought to the ziggurat of Ur were recorded on clay tablets.

ern-day Iraq. The people who founded the first civilization are known as Sumerians. The climate of ancient Sumer, like that of modern Iraq, was harsh. Summers were hot and dry, but spring brought too much water with yearly, unpredictable flooding. Historians like Arnold Toynbee believe that it was the challenge of living in this harsh environment that led the Sumerians to create civilization.

The Sumerians had to learn to build reservoirs to save the flood waters, as well as irrigation systems to channel the water out to the fields during the dry summers. To accomplish this daunting task, they needed centralized direction and cooperation. They also needed specialists who could plan and supervise the engineering projects. Other experts were needed to study the stars and predict the yearly floods. Hence, Sumerian society began to develop a hierarchical structure. Not only did the Sumerians learn to manage the precious water, but they also developed important technological breakthroughs like the wheel and the plow. New kinds of food were introduced, like dates, figs, and olives. These improvements in agriculture meant that farmers produced more than they could eat.

As they were making strides in agriculture, the Sumerians were also finding new ways to work with metal. At the end of the stone age, humans were already making tools and weapons out of copper. In Mesopotamia, however, they began to discover that if copper was melted and mixed with tin, they could produce a new metal that was still easily shaped but was stronger than copper. The new metal was bronze. It made a much sharper and more dangerous weapon as well as a more useful tool. As a result, those in Sumerian towns built walls to protect themselves from these new weapons, but also constructed monumental buildings with the more efficient bronze tools. Historians consider the discovery of bronze so important that they call the following 3,000 years the Bronze Age.

Sumeria was becoming wealthier but also more complex. There were serious problems in managing this changing society. To solve these problems, historians suggest the Sumerians invented writing. At first they kept records by means of tiny clay tokens that represented the objects being counted or traded. However, by 3500 B.C. the system had become unwieldy. It was easier for people to use signs on clay tablets to indicate numbers instead of amassing piles of tokens. Signs were scratched on wet clay tablets that were dried in the sun and then baked in an oven to harden. Thus, writing was born. In time, new words were added through pictographs. Pictographs are simplified pictures that stand for a particular object. Eventually, these evolved into ideograms, which are symbols that are no longer recognizable as specific objects but denote ideas. For example, a picture of an ox would have originally represented just an ox. Later, however, it might be transformed to represent the idea of work. When the Sumerians combined two or more such ideograms, it was possible to communicate more complicated ideas without creating new pictures.

As the centuries passed, these symbols evolved into signs that often looked little like the original pictograph, but the signs became standardized into Sumerian. However, they didn't develop an alphabet where symbols stood for sounds. That came much later. Sumerian pictographs were later learned by neighboring people who adapted it for their own languages. Thus, writing began to spread in the Middle East.

Sumerian was written with a reed stylus, or point, shaped like a triangle. This made wedge-shaped marks. Scholars usually call Sumerian pictographs *cuneiform* because the Latin word for wedge is *cuneus*. Writing Sumerian cuneiform was clumsy and time consuming, and only rigorously-trained scribes had the skill to do it. Nevertheless, writing had a profound effect on Sumerian life. Now economic and commercial records could be kept, along with details of offerings to the gods, important events, and even poetry. After 3000 B.C. historians can learn about the Sumerians in their own words. Armed with their writings and archaeological evidence, we can construct a good estimate of what life was like for the Sumerians.

Discussion

1. Why is writing so important to civilization?
2. What impact did bronze tools have on Sumerian life?
3. Why did civilization appear in Mesopotamia?
4. How is an ideogram different from a pictograph?

Map Activity

Using map B, locate and label the modern states of Iraq, Turkey, Syria, Saudi Arabia, Kuwait, and Iran. Locate and label the modern cities of Baghdad and Al Basrah. Locate and label the Persian Gulf. Locate and label the Tigris and Euphrates Rivers. Finally, using a pen or pencil of a different color, label the area on the northern shore of the Persian Gulf, which was the ancient land of Sumer.

Name _____ Date _____

CHALLENGES

1. What are the characteristics of civilization?

_____

_____

_____

2. When and where did the first civilization appear?

_____

3. What does Arnold Toynbee believe caused civilization to develop?

_____

_____

4. How did irrigation cause specialization?

_____

_____

5. What technological breakthroughs and new kinds of food were developed by the Sumerians?

_____

6. How did the Sumerians make bronze?

_____

7. When did the Bronze Age begin?

_____

8. How did the Sumerians keep records before they discovered writing?

_____

_____

9. What are pictographs?

_____

10. What is cuneiform writing?

_____

9

THE STAIRWAY TO HEAVEN: ANCIENT SUMER

Sumerians leading cattle in a procession to the king's banquet as shown in one panel of the Standard of Ur

The smoke of the burnt offerings drifted down from the temple. Along with it came the voice of the priest calling on the god Utu to bless the people of Uruk and tell them what to do. When the sun reached its zenith overhead, the priest cut the liver out of the sacrificial lamb. He studied its shape and color. Through these the priest and people believed the god spoke to his people. The minutes passed. Below, the city leaders shifted uncomfortably in the bright sun. Eagerly, they awaited the priest's announcement. At last, he emerged from the darkness of the temple. "We must attack our rivals. The god has spoken."

The Sumerians were deeply religious *polytheists* (people who believe in more than one god). These powerful beings created and controlled everything. Utu was the sky-god, Enlil was the air-god, and Ishtar was the goddess of love and war, to name a few. Yet, they were *anthropomorphic* (they looked and acted like humans). Sometimes they were wise and at other times foolish. Each city constructed a temple where the dominant local god was believed to live. This was the *ziggurat.* It was usually the highest building and was located at the center of the town. Made of baked and glazed clay bricks, it was built in the form of seven ascending terraces with a temple on top. The ziggurat was supposed to be a stairway for the god or goddess to descend from heaven to earth. Those who tended the ziggurat controlled great wealth, so the priests, scribes, and temple officials were a major economic power along with the nobility.

Ordinary people usually rented land from either the temple or the nobles. Most were free peasants, but there were also a few slaves, originally captives from beyond the borders of Sumeria. Men and women worked side by side in the fields growing and harvesting dates, flax, wheat, barley, and possibly grapes. Still others worked together tanning hides, grinding grain, or producing pottery. Pottery had been in use since the early Neolithic Age. The invention of the potter's wheel, however, allowed the Sumerians to mass produce new kinds of watertight pottery.

Pottery plays a major role in archaeology. On any archaeological site, the most numerous finds are clay drinking vessels, dishes, storage vases, and water jugs. They are almost always broken. Nevertheless, they are called the alphabet of archaeology. This is because each city had its own shape and decoration for pottery. Also, these characteristics changed over time. When an archaeologist finds a piece of pottery called a shard, he can

10

use his knowledge of where and when that type of pottery was produced to date any other artifacts found at the same level in the ground. In addition, he can often discover what kinds of things were traded and by whom.

One of the best clues to life in ancient Sumer is a wooden panel found in a 4,500-year-old grave in the city of Ur. It is known as the Standard of Ur. Here we can come face to face with the Sumerians. On one side, soldiers and chariots march to battle, fight, and lead away prisoners. On the other side, a procession of Sumerians bring gifts to a victory celebration. Here we can see nobles feasting while a harpist and singer perform. Below, the commoners drive pigs, goats, donkeys, cattle, and sheep to the celebration. Still others carry fish, jewelry, timber, and weapons. We can also study the way the Sumerians saw themselves. They are portrayed as short, squat figures with shaved heads and large eyes.

We know that Sumer was divided up into at least twelve proud and independent city-states. The geography encouraged independence because the cities were divided by desert and swampland. Even though they shared the same language, literature, and religion, they were rivals and often were at war with each other. The main source of conflict was the limited water supply offered by the Tigris and Euphrates Rivers. In times of peace they traded with each other as well as the outside world. From Oman or Sinai they acquired copper, and from Armenia and Nubia, gold.

At first the day-to-day affairs of each city-state were managed by a council of the wealthiest citizens and the temple officials. Less frequently, an assembly of the people met to make more dramatic decisions. Who was allowed to join the assembly and how much freedom of speech they enjoyed we don't know.

However, by the middle of the third millennium B.C. (2500 B.C.), the records begin to reveal the existence of a new force in the life of the city-state. This new force was called the *lugal.* Lugal means "big man." In time these men would rule as kings.

Discussion

1. Why was the ziggurat so important to the Sumerians?
2. How do archaeologists use pottery shards?
3. What conclusions can you draw about life in Sumeria by looking at the Standard of Ur?
4. Describe Sumerian government.

Map Activity

Using map A, locate and label the modern states of Iraq, Turkey, Syria, Saudi Arabia, Kuwait, and Iran. Locate and label the Tigris and Euphrates Rivers and the Sinai Peninsula. Finally, using a pen or pencil of a different color, label the area north of the Persian Gulf between the two cities of the ancient land of Sumer; the ancient city of Ur, which is near the point where the Euphrates River empties into the Persian Gulf; and ancient Nubia, which is in the southern part of Egypt.

Name _____ Date _____

CHALLENGES

1. What is the definition of polytheism?

_____

_____

2. What is the definition of anthropomorphic?

_____

_____

3. What was the shape of a ziggurat?

_____

4. What enabled the Sumerians to produce more and better pottery?

_____

_____

5. What kinds of food did the Sumerians grow?

_____

6. Where was the Standard of Ur discovered? How old is it believed to be?

_____

7. How many separate city-states made up the area called Sumer?

_____

8. What was the main source of conflict between these states?

_____

9. With whom did the Sumerians trade?

_____

10. When did lugals begin to appear?

_____

SARGON THE CONQUEROR: THE RISE OF KINGS

In the bright light of the Mesopotamian morning, the army of Akkad lined up in the plain below the walled city of Uruk. The sun made the polished bronze swords and spears gleam deep orange amongst the dust of the moving foot soldiers and chariots. As soon as the troops had moved into position, a magnificent chariot carrying a black-bearded leader galloped out in front. He surveyed his troops and then raised his sword as a sign to begin the attack. The Akkadian army surged forward with scaling ladders and battering rams. After several hours of bloody fighting on the walls, Uruk fell. The captured king, Lugalzaggisi, was dragged from his palace and forced to fall on his knees before the conqueror. Within days of capture, the walls of the city were pulled down so that Uruk could never again defy Akkad. Another city had fallen to the conqueror Sargon.

Sargon of Akkad

The Mesopotamian kings were primarily warriors, and the constant warfare between the city-states gave them plenty of opportunity to practice their skills. Several warrior-kings tried to unite or conquer all the Sumerian city-states, but the most successful was Sargon. He controlled all of the Sumerian cities and even marched into new lands beyond. He penetrated Anatolia in the north and sailed down the Euphrates to the Persian Gulf. At the end of his reign, he could boast that he ruled over what he thought was "the peoples of all lands" or "the four quarters of the earth." To control his vast empire, he replaced the kings he conquered with his own relatives whom he could trust to remain loyal. As we saw above, he crushed the rebellion of conquered cities ruthlessly. Sargon also was the first king to claim the right of dynastic succession. This means that Sargon's sons and grandsons claimed the right to be king because they were his descendants. Later kings even claimed to be gods.

Yet Sargon had not been born a king. As a small child his mother abandoned him to the Euphrates River in a reed basket. He was saved and raised by a water-drawer. Through the help of a priestess of Ishtar, the goddess of love and war, he became cup-bearer to the king of Kish, one of the many small city-states that made up Sumeria. Eventually he rose to the position of lugal or king of Akkad through his own efforts. As a result, he was sensitive to doubts about his right to rule. To silence such questions, he chose the name Sargon, which means "the king is legitimate."

Like other kings, he also claimed that he was the representative of the many Sumerian gods on Earth. Therefore, he appointed his daughter Enheduanna the high

13

priestess of the moon goddess Nanna and the heaven-god An. Nanna was the city goddess of Ur and An the city god of Uruk. These were the chief cities of Sumeria. By joining them together through his daughter, he helped to unite his lands. Enheduanna's surviving portrait reveals a somber woman deeply aware of her responsibility. She was well educated in the Sumerian language and was a brilliant writer. She wrote two beautiful hymns to Nanna. As a result, she became the first known author in history and a valuable supporter to her father.

Sargon's sons and grandsons followed him onto the throne and continued to expand the Akkadian Empire into Palestine and Syria. Like Sargon, all of the Sumerian kings after him appointed their daughters to the highest religious post in the land, the High Priestess of Nanna and An. The sculptures and bronze casts of these kings reveal stern-faced, confident men with long, curled beards, carefully arranged hair, and rippling muscles. One of the most famous portraits is the stele of Naram-Sin, the grandson of Sargon. A stele is an upright stone slab with a picture carved into it in relief. Relief sculptures are flat surfaces with images of figures projecting up from the surface. Reliefs are the most common kind of Mesopotamian sculpture. Naram-Sin ruled for 56 years and carried out many of the reforms begun by his grandfather. The steles also bare witness to the continued flowering of the arts under him and his successors.

The dynasty lasted over 100 years before collapsing once again into smaller city-states. In that time the bonds between the different cities had been strengthened, and Sumerian culture had spread to other neighboring peoples.

Discussion

1. Why would Sargon claim that he was the representative of all of the many Sumerian gods?
2. Why did Sargon and his descendants have themselves portrayed (in masks and reliefs) the way they did?
3. How did Sargon deal with his enemies?

Map Activity

Using map B, locate and label the modern states of Iraq, Iran, Kuwait, Turkey, and Syria. Locate and label the Tigris and Euphrates Rivers. Finally, using a pen or pencil of a different color, label the area between the two rivers that is known as Mesopotamia; the ancient city of Akkad that was located north of where the two rivers are the closest to each other; the ancient city of Uruk that was close to the modern city of Assamawah in Iraq; Ur, which was 50 miles southeast of Uruk on the other side of the river; and Anatolia, which is modern-day central Turkey.

Name _____ Date _____

CHALLENGES

1. How did Sargon rise to power?

_____

_____

2. What did Sargon claim he controlled?

_____

3. In reality what did he control?

_____

4. What new lands did Sargon penetrate?

_____

5. How did Sargon try to silence questions about his rise to power?

_____

6. Who was the first known author in history?

_____

7. What are relief sculptures?

_____

_____

8. How long did Sargon's dynasty last?

_____

9. What impact did Sargon's empire have on Mesopotamia?

_____

_____

10. What impact did Sargon's empire have on neighboring people?

_____

_____

GILGAMESH BATTLES WITH DEATH: THE GODS OF ANCIENT SUMER

There was a time when Enlil, the most powerful of the gods, became disgusted with humankind. He decided to send a flood to cleanse the world. The punishment seemed too harsh to Enki, the god of water. He visited Utnapishtim, a man known for his goodness, and advised him to build a giant boat to ride out the flood. In addition to his family, Utnapishtim made room on his boat for pairs of all the animals of the land and air. For seven days and seven nights the boat was tossed on the swirling waters. On the eighth day, the rains stopped and Utnapishtim opened a hatch to let the light from the sun fall upon his face. Eventually, the boat hit dry land and Utnapishtim released all the animals to repopulate the earth.

Enki, the Sumerian god of water, is portrayed with fish streaming about his shoulders. Since the Sumerians feared both droughts and floods, Enki was one of their most important gods.

This story is from the Epic of Gilgamesh. An epic is a story of heroic deeds, usually written in the form of a long poem. The main character was the incredibly strong king of Uruk named Gilgamesh. Most of the epic was taken up describing his youthful rivalry and then close friendship with Enkidu. After enjoying several adventures together, Enkidu unexpectedly died, leaving Gilgamesh broken-hearted. While trying to come to terms with his friend's death, Gilgamesh searched the world over for the secret of immortality. He failed to find it and returned home to record his travels on a stone. Only by doing this did he finally achieve immortality. On his adventures he visited Utnapishtim who told him the story of the great flood. Eventually Gilgamesh accepted his friend's death and his own inevitable end. The story is typical of Sumerian and Babylonian religion and literature. Living in a harsh natural environment with little rain, unpredictable rivers, and constant warfare, the inhabitants of Mesopotamia were pessimistic about life and death. The gods, who were depicted in human form, were demanding, and people believed that they were merely the servants of the gods. Failure to please the gods was thought to bring about punishment. In fact, it was Enkidu's rejection of the advances of Ishtar, the goddess of love, that caused his death. The people were in constant fear of the gods and believed that after death only a dreary eternal existence as unhappy ghosts awaited them. The epic of Gilgamesh is also interesting to historians because it contains not only a story of a great flood, but also stories similar to the Biblical accounts of the Garden of Eden and Job.

Although the Epic of Gilgamesh was written by a Sumerian, the oldest surviving versions are written in Babylonian. The Babylonians borrowed the epic along with much else. Their kings followed in Sargon's footsteps by conquering much of Mesopotamia. They also set up a new capital in the south called Babylon. The Babylonians not only absorbed, but also built upon the achievements of the Sumerians.

The Babylonians used the Sumerian mathematical system based on powers of sixty for business, engineering, and astronomy. Even today we still divide hours by sixty. The Babylonians were especially interested in astronomy as part of their greater interest in astrology. They believed that by studying the movements of the stars, they could predict the future. Soon they were producing accurate maps of the movements of major constellations, stars, and planets. Babylonian physicians also learned to use various plants as medicine and even performed difficult surgeries like Caesarean sections.

The Babylonians are probably best known for their law codes, especially Hammurabi's Code. It is named after a great king who collected almost 300 rulings on all aspects of Babylonian life. Hammurabi hoped to unify his Sumerian subjects by offering them a collection of legal decisions rendered during his reign. Law was important to the people of the early Middle East as a way to bring order out of chaos. Thus, it was important to religion as well as government.

The code is an excellent source for historians on life in ancient Babylonia. From the code, we can tell that society was divided into three classes: slaves, free people who owned land, and others who were free but worked for the land owners. Rights were often class-based. We also know that debt was a widespread problem and often forced people to sell their daughters into slavery. Nevertheless, women could own and inherit property and testify in court. Many of the punishments listed in the code seem harsh to us. For example, the code requires that if a free man destroyed the eye of another free man, the culprit would lose his eye, too. We also know that children could be punished for the crimes of their fathers. Yet, Hammurabi's code is remarkable as evidence of the growing sophistication of Mesopotamian civilization.

Discussion

1. The Sumerians didn't believe in a happy afterlife. What impact do you believe this would have on Sumerian society?
2. What does Hammurabi's code tell us about Babylonian society?
3. Why do you think astrology was so important to the Babylonians?
4. What conclusions can you make about Sumerian society from the Epic of Gilgamesh?

Map Activity

Using map B, locate and label the modern states of Iraq, Iran, Kuwait, Turkey, and Saudi Arabia. Locate and label the Tigris and Euphrates Rivers. Finally, using a pen or pencil of a different color, label ancient Sumer, which was located between the two rivers and north of the Persian Gulf; the ancient city of Uruk, which was near the modern-day city of Assamawah in Iraq; the ancient city of Babylon, which was located on the Euphrates where the two rivers are closest to each other; and (in a different color from Sumer) Babylonia, which covered the area between the two rivers south to the Persian Gulf.

Name _____ Date _____

CHALLENGES

1. What familiar stories do we find in the Epic of Gilgamesh?

_____

_____

2. Why were the Mesopotamians so pessimistic?

_____

_____

3. What is an epic?

_____

4. Who were the Babylonians?

_____

5. What was the Babylonian mathematical system based on?

_____

6. Why were the Babylonians interested in astronomy?

_____

_____

7. What are the Babylonians best known for?

_____

8. What were the three classes of Babylonian society?

_____

9. What rights did Babylonian women have?

_____

_____

10. What was the punishment for destroying the eye of another person?

_____

_____

THE GIFT OF THE NILE: THE RISE OF ANCIENT EGYPT

The Narmer Slate Palette commemorates the conquest of Lower Egypt by Upper Egypt.

At the beginning of the history of ancient Egypt is the mystery of the Narmer Slate Palette, the oldest surviving image of an historic person identified by name. On one side, it shows a mighty king wearing the crown of Upper Egypt, the area to the south of the Nile Delta. He is about to kill a bearded enemy while others flee. To his right, a falcon, the symbol of Upper Egypt, holds the head of a vanquished foe while sitting upon papyrus reeds in the shape of the Nile Delta. On the other side, a king wearing the crown of Lower Egypt, the area of the Nile Delta, marches in procession preceded by four standard-bearers and an important official. Dead bodies with their heads cut off are piled to his left. Below that scene, two beasts with serpent-like necks intertwine, and below that a bull destroys a city. What do these symbols mean? It is impossible to know for sure, but many archaeologists believe that it commemorates the conquest of Lower Egypt by Upper Egypt, thus uniting Egypt under one ruler.

Archaeologists also know that around the same time, monumental architecture and writing appeared. It is uncertain whether the Egyptians invented these things or learned them from the Mesopotamians. In any case, by 2700 B.C. the Egyptians had created the sophisticated and vibrant civilization of the Old Kingdom. Historians have divided Egyptian history into three distinct eras: the Old Kingdom (2686–2160 B.C.), the Middle Kingdom (2040–1633 B.C.), and the New Kingdom (1558–1085 B.C.). The eras are divided by years during which the central government broke down. These spaces between the kingdoms are known as Intermediate Periods.

The ancient Greek historian, Herodotus, described Egypt as "the gift of the Nile." His statement is accurate. Like Mesopotamia, Egyptian civilization was shaped by its close proximity to a river. Egypt was also dry and relied on irrigation to collect and distribute water. The Nile served as an avenue for transport to Egyptian cities. Here food, fuel, and the building materials that were used to construct the pyramids could be transported. Water from the Nile could also be channeled to arid lands away from the river all year long. Almost all Egyptians lived in the narrow belt and fan-shaped delta of fertile land shaped by the Nile. Because the river runs from south to north, the Egyptians called the land in the south Upper Egypt, while the delta in the north they called Lower Egypt. Egypt and Mesopotamia are different, however. Unlike the dangerous and unpredictable Tigris and Euphrates, the Nile is remarkably regular. Its annual floods were not only predictable, but were looked forward to by the Egyptians to bring water and fresh, black soil from upriver to rejuvenate the land. As a result, Egyptian agriculture was the most successful of the ancient world. Much later, when Egypt came under the control of Rome, the Romans relied on the abundance of Egyptian agriculture to feed much of the Roman Empire.

The Egyptians enjoyed other advantages as well. Egypt was rich in natural resources. The stems of the papyrus plant, which grew along the banks of the river, could be dried and pressed to make a kind of paper. Copper and turquoise were abundant in the Sinai peninsula and gold could be found in the desert east of the river. Finally, limestone, which was so important for the many building projects, was quarried in Lower Egypt. The Nile River is protected on the east and west by deserts too vast for most invaders to cross. Thus Egypt developed a homogeneous civilization of its own, developing without much outside interference. Although the Egyptians traded with Mesopotamia and Syria, there is little sign that this contact affected Egyptian culture. Nor did Egypt suffer from chronic warfare over scarcity. In Egypt there was plenty of water and rich farm land. Because of these advantages, the Egyptians were more optimistic than the Sumerians. For instance, they believed in an afterlife as good as, if not better than, the present. Each year the Nile brought new life to Egyptian agriculture, so they believed death must only be a brief season before an afterlife in the next world. Historians also believe that faith in the static or unchanging nature of life helped to promote the idea of a single, all-powerful king who watched over his people and gave them all they needed. He was known as the pharaoh. This ruler supplied Egyptians with a strong central government, an elaborate bureaucracy to manage the complex irrigation system, and a living symbol of order to worship. The stability of life also gives Egyptian history remarkable continuity. Religion, fashion, language, art, and social tradition remained basically unchanged. A day in the life of an Egyptian during the reign of king Narmer was very similar to a day in the life of an Egyptian living almost 3,000 years later at the end of the period we call ancient Egypt.

Discussion

1. Why do you think archaeologists believe that the Narmer Slate Palette commemorates the conquest of Lower Egypt by Upper Egypt?
2. Why was there so much continuity in Egyptian life?
3. Why would historians divide Egyptian history into three eras?

Map Activity

Using map D, locate and label the modern states of Egypt, Israel, Jordan, Sudan, and Libya. Also locate and label the Sinai Peninsula, the Nile River, the Nile Delta, the Red Sea, the Mediterranean Sea, the Gulf of Aqaba, the Gulf of Suez, and the modern Suez Canal. Finally, using a pen or pencil of a different color, locate and label Upper and Lower Egypt and the ancient capital, Memphis, which was located at the southern end of the Nile Delta on the west side of the river.

Name _____ Date _____

CHALLENGES

1. Where is Upper Egypt?

_____

2. How were Upper and Lower Egypt united?

_____

_____

3. What are the three eras of Egyptian history?

_____

4. Why did Herodotus describe Egypt as the gift of the Nile?

_____

_____

5. How is the Nile different from the Tigris and Euphrates Rivers?

_____

6. Why is Egyptian history more peaceful than Mesopotamian?

_____

_____

7. Why did the Egyptians believe in a good afterlife?

_____

_____

8. How were the Egyptians dependent upon the flooding of the Nile?

_____

_____

9. What promoted the idea of the pharaoh?

_____

10. How is Egyptian history noted for its continuity?

_____

_____

THE GLORIES OF EGYPT: THE PYRAMIDS AND THE SPHINX

Ask the average person today to name three things about ancient Egypt, and they will probably answer "pyramids, the Sphinx, and mummies." If asked why the Egyptians erected the colossal pyramids and the Sphinx and mummified the bodies of the dead, they might give a good answer. But if asked how it was done, they will be stumped because we can only guess about their methods.

The Egyptians were strong believers in life after death. They believed a complete body was needed to house the soul, or *ka,* so they developed a process to keep the body preserved. The bodies

Funeral barges transport the body of the pharaoh to his pyramid by way of a canal that branches off from the Nile.

of the wealthier Egyptians were taken to the City of the Dead, where those trained in the procedure turned the body into a mummy. Those who knew the secret were not going to reveal their methods in writing because they did not want competition. The procedure was rather gruesome, and we have a good idea of how it was done, but the chemicals used to preserve the mummy remain a mystery. We know it was a long process because the time between death and burial was 70 days.

The great Sphinx sits proudly near the pyramid of the pharaoh Khafre and was built with blocks of stone remaining after that pyramid was completed. The lion body is 240 feet long, and the human head wearing the royal headpiece rises 66 feet above the base. It is certain that the features of the face are those of Khafre and that the Sphinx was built to honor him. Later, pharaohs used the Sphinx as a symbol of their god-given right to rule. The Sphinx today suffers from abuse by man and desert sandstorms, but considering that it was built between c.a. 2575 and 2467 B.C., it reflects well on its builders.

The most massive projects of the Middle Eastern world were the pyramids. They were built to honor a pharaoh and provide him with a tomb worthy of his glory. Work on the pyramid began while the pharaoh was alive and continued many years after his death. Around the bases of the pyramids, large palaces, temples, and storerooms were built. Here priests would oversee the worship of the pharaoh's spirit long after he was dead. Outside the temple complex, much smaller pyramids for the queens were constructed, and beyond those were flat tombs called *mastabas* for the pharaoh's officials. In the Old Kingdom, an afterlife was reserved for only the pharaoh and his officials. The pharaoh was perceived as a god. He was considered the child of the Sun god Re. This god-king ruled over his realm according to the principle of *ma'at,* which meant order, justice, and truth.

The 80 pyramids of Egypt were located west of the Nile River and in the desert beyond irrigated land. Most of the large pyramids were built between the third and sixth

22

dynasties, in the period of the Old Kingdom, all within 20 miles of the ancient capital of Memphis at a place called Gizeh. Herodotus, the Greek historian, estimated that 100,000 men worked for 20 years in the seasons between Nile floods to complete the Great Pyramid.

The base of each was the same. All were square at the base. The so-called Great Pyramid built in honor of Khufu (Cheops) had a base 755 feet long and stood 481 feet tall. Construction was so precise that the measurements at the base were correct within six-tenths of an inch. The angles of the sides make an almost perfect triangle.

Construction involved some very difficult geometric calculations, all made without the aid of a computer. Consider the problems. Everything had to be built perfectly level, otherwise it would never look right. Using water in trenches to test levels, they were so accurate in building the Great Pyramid that the northwest corner stands only a half inch lower than the southeast corner. Then they had to find the rock to cut and move it from the quarry 600 miles away to the building site. Once there, groups of 18 to 20 men pulled the two-and-a-half-ton stone block up a ramp until it reached its proper spot on the pyramid.

Since the purpose was to create a place for the pharaoh's body to lie in splendor, a burial chamber was built deep inside the pyramid. Included there were the Pyramid Texts, instructions to the pharaoh on how to guide his vessel through the underworld to the sky to Re, the Sun god. A passageway was constructed so the workers assigned to prepare the chamber could climb to the tomb. After their work was done, it was their route for leaving. To keep grave robbers out, stones were dropped in place when the workers left. These passageways created the threat of internal collapse that might bring down the whole structure. This required heavy granite slabs to be laid over the king's chamber.

Not all pyramids looked exactly alike. The first one attempted was built for King Djoser and was designed by his brilliant architect, Imhotep. It was called the "stepped pyramid" because its sides resemble six steps climbing to the top. The pyramid of King Snefru is called the "bent pyramid" because the angle was steeper at the base than in the top half. The later pyramids also differed in size and the types of stone used.

The monuments of Egypt stand today as testimony to Egypt's religion, knowledge of mathematics, skill in building huge structures, and the glory of the pharaohs.

Discussion

1. If there were an American Sphinx, whose face do you think should be carved on it? Why?
2. How would the Egyptians have felt about cremation? Why?
3. Suppose a bill were proposed in Congress to spend $2 billion on a pyramid honoring an American president. What would be the reaction?
4. Look at pictures of the Washington, Jefferson, and Lincoln memorials and compare them with the pyramids. Why do we give such small honor to our leaders?

Map Activity

Using map D, locate and label the modern states of Egypt, Israel, Jordan, Sudan, and Saudi Arabia. Also locate and label the Sinai Peninsula, the Nile River, the Red Sea, the Mediterranean Sea, and the Gulf of Suez. Also locate and label the modern cities of Aswan, Asyt, and Gaza. Finally, using a pen or pencil of a different color, locate and label Gizeh, which is just south of modern-day Cairo on the west side of the river.

Name _____ Date _____

CHALLENGES

1. Why didn't the experts at the City of the Dead write down the chemical formula for their preservatives?

_____

_____

2. How long did it take from death to burial?

_____

3. What is the ka?

_____

4. What has caused deterioration of the Sphinx?

_____

_____

5. What is a mastaba?

_____

_____

6. What is ma'at?

_____

_____

7. Where are the most impressive pyramids located?

_____

8. How many men and how much time did Herodotus think it took to build the Great Pyramid?

_____

9. What did they use to measure to be sure that every stone was level?

_____

10. What was the purpose of the Pyramid Text?

_____

_____

THE EYE OF HORUS: THE EGYPTIAN GODS

Osiris, the god who brought civilization to Egypt and ruled over the earth, had an evil brother named Seth. Seth was the god of storms, chaos, and the desert. He was jealous of his brother's power and his beautiful wife, the enchantress Isis. One day Seth murdered his brother and scattered Osiris's dismembered body throughout Egypt. Isis mourned for her husband, and her tears were so great that they created the Nile. That night, Isis, although devastated by the death of her husband, secretly collected and reassembled the various parts of his body. She revived him by mummifying his body, and they produced a falcon-headed son named Horus. Osiris, however, had discovered the afterlife, and he returned there.

As Horus grew into manhood, he was determined to avenge the death of his father and win back the rule of the earth. Also, with Seth's victory over Osiris, the land had fallen

Horus, the son of the Egyptian gods Isis and Osiris, was often portrayed as a falcon.

into chaos and was infertile. Horus felt that he must bring the land back to life. At last he faced Seth in a terrible three-day battle. The lightning was Horus's spear, and the thunder was the cry of the wounded Seth roaring in pain. Horus was victorious, and the land once again bloomed with life. Horus, however, lost an eye, which entered the sky as the Moon. According to Egyptian belief, every pharaoh ruled on Earth as Horus, and when he died, became the lord of the afterlife as Osiris. The dangerous Seth was forever exiled to the north.

Egyptian religion is complex. There were overlapping and often contradictory beliefs, myths, and practices. Often the myths changed over time or merged with other myths. For example, sometimes Egyptian mythology taught that the sky was a goddess named Nut who stretched over the earth, but at other times they believed it was a gigantic cow. Sometimes the Nile flowed from Isis's tears, and at other times it flowed from the dismembered body of Osiris. Six different gods personify the Moon. The tendency to combine contradictory beliefs is called *syncretism*. The Egyptians weren't troubled by these contradictions. To them, these different beliefs were all valid ways of describing nature.

Egyptian gods took many forms. From earliest times the most important god was Re or Ra, the god of the Sun. Other gods were worshipped only in certain cities or regions, but Re was worshipped by all Egyptians. In the Old Kingdom he became the official national god. However, the Egyptians eventually worshipped over 2,000 different gods. The most common forms were animals. Horus was portrayed as a falcon; Anubis, the judge of the dead, had the head of a jackal; Hathor, the goddess of love and childbirth, had the head of a cow. Thoth, the scribe of the gods, took the form of a baboon or an ibis, a bird often found on the Nile. Seth had the head of a strange, perhaps prehistoric, animal that even puzzled the Egyptians. Other gods combined parts of many animals. Tawert, a goddess of childbirth, embodied parts of a hippopotamus, crocodile, and lioness. Live animals associated with gods were often kept and worshipped. For example, crocodiles representing Sobek, one of the gods of the sun, earth, and water, were worshipped and lived a life of luxury in the temple pool of Crocodilopolis. When they died, they were mummified and placed in tombs like humans.

Sometimes the Egyptians turned real people into gods. The pharaohs were worshipped while still alive. A few pharaohs or great men were so popular that they were worshipped after they died. For example, the architect of the first pyramid, Imhotep, was considered a god of wisdom.

Most ancient Egyptians had only limited access to temples where the gods were worshipped. They might only see the statues at festival time when the priests would bring out the divine images and carry them around the city on their shoulders. However, ordinary Egyptians could always express their devotion to a god or goddess by possessing small amulets or statuettes. Sometimes, furniture was decorated with the face of a god or goddess. For example, the image of Bes, one of the gods of the family, often decorated eating utensils or children's cradles. Also, there were parts of the temples set aside for persons who wanted to make special appeals to the gods. Sometimes, the gods were invoked for specific purposes. Water poured over the image of Hor-pa-khered was believed to have special power to cure poisonous bites and stings.

Discussion

1. What does the Osiris myth tell you about what was important to Egyptians?
2. Explain how it was possible for the Egyptians to be syncretists.
3. Why did the Egyptians give their gods the heads of animals?

Map Activity

Using map D, locate and label the modern states of Egypt, Israel, Libya, Sudan, and Jordan. Also locate and label the Nile River, the Red Sea, the Mediterranean Sea, and the Gulf of Aqaba. Also locate and label the modern cities of Cairo, Alexandria, and Port Said. Finally, using a pen or pencil of a different color, locate and label ancient Memphis, which was just south of modern-day Cairo and Crocodilopolos, which was located between the Nile and the southern shore of Lake Faiyum.

Name _____ Date _____

CHALLENGES

1. Who was Osiris?

_____

2. Who was Seth?

_____

3. According to Egyptian mythology, where did the Nile come from?

_____

_____

4. According to Egyptian mythology, where did the Moon come from?

_____

_____

5. What is syncretism?

_____

_____

6. Give an example of syncretism.

_____

_____

7. How was Horus portrayed?

_____

8. How many different Egyptian gods were there?

_____

9. Who was Sobek?

_____

_____

10. Who was Imhotep?

_____

_____

GRAVE ROBBERS: THE END OF THE OLD KINGDOM

At last the rock gave way and the tomb robbers found themselves in a cool, dark passage. They cautiously moved in what seemed to be the direction of the center of the pyramid. Their tiny oil lamps lit up the walls of the passage brightly decorated with inscriptions, gods, and images of the dead pharaoh. At last they came to a huge, sealed door. They immediately set about smashing it with their pick-axes. The door was so thick that they had to return to the passage several nights in a row. However, with the grounds and temples around the pyramid now abandoned, it was possible to make their way back into the tomb. It would never have

Pharaohs were depicted in statues, busts, reliefs, and many other types of artwork. The pharaoh was worshiped as a god on Earth.

been this easy even a few years before, but now no one bothered to guard the tombs. Finally, the door collapsed and they pushed into the outer chamber of the pharaoh's tomb. Although the light of their oil lamps was pale and small, it nevertheless flashed on the surface of objects of gold and precious stones beyond their wildest dreams. Centuries later when archaeologists would enter this and all of the other pyramids, they would find them empty.

The Old Kingdom came to an end with the reign of Pepi II. He was eight years old when be became pharaoh, and he ruled for the next 90 years. Pepi II was never a brilliant ruler, and he probably lost interest in the job by the time of his old age. At that time, rulers were supposed to be above worry, so the old pharaoh left details of state to be handled by others, giving influence and power to those who ruled in the name of the pharaoh. When Pepi II died, so did centralized power. Egypt entered an era of rulers who were called pharaohs, but commanded no respect. One did not need to be a member of the pharaoh's family to become a high official anymore. The short reigns of these pharaohs indicate that the situation was unstable with one pharaoh overthrown by another.

Historians and archaeologists are uncertain why the Old Kingdom fell. One possible explanation offered is that the cost of constructing so many pyramids for the pharaohs of the Old Kingdom exhausted the resources of the state. Pharaohs borrowed money from nobles in return for land or special privileges. In time, the provincial governors, called monarchs, became so powerful that their offices became hereditary, and they could challenge the pharaoh's power. As the pharaoh's power declined, there was no one to administer justice or manage irrigation. At the same time, the monsoon rains in Ethiopia, which filled the Nile River with water, slackened. As a result, Egypt was swept with drought and famine. In addition to ransacked tombs, the surviving sources from the period paint a picture of anarchy with brother fighting brother, cannibalism, government files thrown into the streets, and Egypt divided between two opposing kingdoms. This is the First Intermediate Period. It came to an end when the country was at last reunified under pharaoh Nebhepetre Mentuhotep in 2040 B.C.

The strain of the First Intermediate Period had a profound effect on the Egyptians. As a result, many things were different in the Middle Kingdom than they had been in the Old Kingdom. The new pharaohs abandoned the old capital of Memphis for a new one further south called Thebes. They began to make their sons co-rulers so that they could gain experience ruling and be sure that no one would challenge their right to rule when the old pharaoh died. They were determined to avoid the anarchy of the First Intermediate Period.

Also, the attitude toward the pharaoh changed. No longer was he the remote god-king of the Old Kingdom. Instead, the pharaoh now appeared more like the good shepherd of his people. This difference is apparent in the statuary of the two kingdoms. In the Old Kingdom, the pharaoh is usually portrayed as indifferent and serene. In the Middle Kingdom, the more realistic statues show rulers with concerned and even worried looks on their faces. These portraits reflect the general mood of the times. The writings from the Middle Kingdom show an inward-looking and serious Egyptian society interested in a sense of common humanity and ethics.

Discussion

1. What were some of the many possible causes of the First Intermediate Period?
2. How do you explain the fact that the Middle Kingdom was different from the Old Kingdom?
3. Why do you think the pharaohs wanted to move their capital to a new place?

Map Activity

Using map A, locate and label Egypt, Sudan, Ethiopia, Saudi Arabia, Cyprus, Lebanon, and Yemen. Also locate and label the Red Sea, the Mediterranean Sea, the Nile River, the Sinai Peninsula, and the modern cities of Jiddah, Mecca, Khartoum, Tel Aviv, and Beirut. Finally, using a pen or pencil of a different color, locate and label ancient Memphis, which was just south of modern-day Cairo, and ancient Thebes, which was located just across the river from modern-day Luxor.

Name _____ Date _____

CHALLENGES

1. Who were monarchs?

_____

2. Who was Nebhepetre Mentuhotep?

_____

3. In what year did the First Intermediate Period end?

_____

4. How might the pyramids have lead to the fall of the Old Kingdom?

_____

_____

5. How did the monsoon rains in Ethiopia help to bring the Old Kingdom to an end?

_____

_____

6. What kind of a picture do the surviving sources from the First Intermediate Period portray?

_____

_____

7. Where was the new capital of the Middle Kingdom?

_____

8. How did the pharaohs of the Middle Kingdom try to avoid anarchy in the future?

_____

_____

9. Why do archaeologists believe that the pharaoh of the Middle Kingdom was more like a good shepherd to his people than a distant god-king?

_____

_____

10. What do the writings from the Middle Kingdom reveal about Egyptian society?

_____

_____

THE TEST OF THE AFTERLIFE: THE MIDDLE KINGDOM

The wall painting shows the nobleman Ptah-Amun appearing before Osiris and the other gods of the underworld. Anubis, the jackal-headed god, steps forward to weigh Ptah's heart. On one side of the scale he places the heart. On the other side he places a feather which represents *ma'at* or truth. If the scale is balanced, the soul of Ptah is admitted into the afterlife, but if the scale tips, the *ka,* or soul, is destroyed by a fierce beast called the Devourer of Souls. Meanwhile, Thoth, the baboon-headed god, records the event. Ptah's soul passes the test because in the next wall painting we see him being welcomed into the beautiful, green garden of the afterlife. Similar images appear in tomb after tomb of the Middle Kingdom.

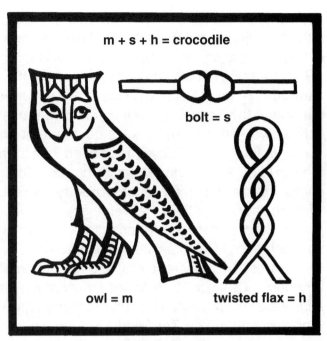

These symbols represent the three consonants of the Egyptian word for crocodile, which may have been pronounced "meseh," "miseh," or "emseh" after vowels were added.

The new interest in ethics or right and wrong meant that the afterlife became open to other people besides the pharaoh. Even ordinary Egyptians, if they could afford to buy the right inscriptions of funeral prayers and spells, could be assured of an eternal life. This was made easier by the existence of paper, or papyrus. This came from weaving fibers from the papyrus plant which grew in abundance along the Nile.

On the papyrus, the Egyptians used *hieroglyphic writing* to record these prayers and spells. Hieroglyphic writing was done by drawing pictures. Before the Old Kingdom, when Egyptians first began to use hieroglyphics, the pictures were probably supposed to mean what they represented. For example, a picture of a basket meant a basket. As time went by, however, they found this too limiting and complicated. For example, to convey the idea of walking, the Egyptians could draw a man walking, but could not show someone walking slowly. The Egyptians found that they could be more precise if they used pictures to represent sounds. Then it would be possible to spell out things that would be difficult to convey by pictures.

There were 600 different hieroglyphics representing the sounds found in the spoken Egyptian language. These hieroglyphics were used the same way we use the letters of the alphabet. For example, the hieroglyph showing a hand represented the sound of the letter "d." The hieroglyph of a cobra represented the sound of the letter "j." Some hieroglyphs, however, continued to mean what their pictures represented. The hieroglyph showing an ox meant just that. The hieroglyph showing an eye weeping meant "to cry."

The Egyptian scribes also had another method of writing called hieratic. This was a shorthand for administration, accounting, and legal documents. For this scribes abbreviated hieroglyphic signs representing the most commonly used combinations. As time went by, hieratic came to be even more abbreviated. As a result of contacts between Egypt and Greece, it finally evolved into an alphabet known as Coptic. The Coptic Christian Church in Egypt today still uses the script for its liturgy.

Most Egyptians couldn't read or write hieroglyphics. Reading and writing were skills learned only by the scribes. Like other occupations in ancient Egypt such as farming or carpentry, the knowledge of the scribe was passed along from father to son. Many of the scribes worked in the pharaoh's government and became powerful men.

In their tombs, Egyptians buried with them all that they believed they would need in the next life. Archaeologists have not only found papyrus scrolls containing prayers and spells, but also historical records, poetry, technical treatises in mathematics and medicine, wisdom stories, letters between government officials, business contracts, and royal proclamations. It is largely because of the survival of these papyrus records that we know so much about Egyptian life during that time.

Most of the great works of Egyptian literature were written during the Middle Kingdom. The society that they describe was peaceful, balanced, and refined. This impression is born out by the funeral architecture. It is smaller and more human than the Old Kingdom's pyramids. The Middle Kingdom pharaoh, Mentuhotep, built a beautiful mortuary temple for himself at Deir el-Bahre. Two colonnaded terraces lead up to a small, graceful pyramid at the top.

Discussion

1. Why did the Egyptians feel that they had to improve upon hieroglyphics?
2. What evidence is there from the Middle Kingdom to show that Egyptians during this period were more concerned with ethics?
3. Why would scribes often become powerful men?

Map Activity

Using map D, locate and label the modern states of Israel, Libya, Sudan, Saudi Arabia, and Jordan. Also locate and label the Red Sea, the Nile River, the Mediterranean Sea, Lake Nasser, the Western Desert, Lake Faiyum, and the modern cities of El Mansura, El Arish, Elat, and Amman. Finally, using a pen or pencil of a different color, locate and label ancient Memphis, which was just south of modern-day Cairo; Gizeh, which was just across the river from Cairo; and Thebes, which was just across the river from modern Luxor.

Name _____ Date _____

CHALLENGES

1. What is weighed on the scale against the ka?

_____

2. What was the name of the baboon-headed god?

_____

3. Where did papyrus come from?

_____

_____

4. How are hieroglyphics made?

_____

_____

5. How many kinds of hieroglyphs are found in the Egyptian language?

_____

6. What did the hieroglyph showing a hand represent?

_____

7. Who did all of the reading and writing in ancient Egypt?

_____

8. How was the knowledge of writing passed on?

_____

9. What kinds of writings did Egyptians place in their tombs?

_____

_____

_____

10. Why do we know so much about Egyptian life?

_____

_____

_____

THE WAR CHARIOTS OF THE HYKSOS: THE END OF THE MIDDLE KINGDOM

Only the far-off land of Punt produced the valuable frankincense and myrrh so necessary to Egyptian religious ceremonies. Yet Punt was located on the east coast of Africa, probably near present-day Somalia, far from the Nile River Valley. To reach it, traders had to plan an eight-day trek across the blistering eastern desert to the Red Sea. Once they arrived at the coast, they re-assembled a boat that they had carried. From here they sailed down to Punt. After returning with the cargo, they began the arduous journey back across the desert to the Nile.

Egyptian women wore elaborate jewelry and clothing and used a wide variety of products for cosmetics.

Punt wasn't the only foreign land visited by the Egyptians of the Middle Kingdom. Traders also traveled to Nubia in the south to bring back gold. In the northeast, Egyptian ships sailed to Byblos on the coast of Lebanon to bring back cedar logs. From the island of Crete across the Mediterranean came olive oil. Imported products were necessary for many aspects of Egyptian life.

Clothing was an important sign of status. The nobles adorned themselves in long pleated fabric and heavy bracelets and necklaces made of gold, turquoise, and lapis lazuli. Egyptian women used a wide range of products for cosmetics. They wore wigs made of human hair kept in place by beeswax and perfumed by cones of hippopotamus fat. For eye shadow they used green malachite, and for rouge and fingernail polish they used red ocher.

The Middle Kingdom pharaohs were interested not only in improving Egyptian life through foreign trade, but they also hoped to avoid some of the problems that had led to the collapse of the Old Kingdom. The powerful provincial governors who had defied the Old Kingdom pharaohs were weakened. Also, a gigantic irrigation project moved water from the Nile to a natural depression called Lake Faiyum where it could be stored for use during the dry season.

The Middle Kingdom is also known for its literature. One of the best-known stories is the "Tale of the Shipwrecked Sailor." On a voyage to Punt, an Egyptian official is shipwrecked on a magical island ruled over by a serpent. The serpent turns out to be the only survivor of a mysterious object from the heavens that crashed into the earth. After loading the shipwrecked sailor down with gifts, the serpent predicts that the sailor will soon be rescued.

The Middle Kingdom, however, was severely weakened by excessive flooding of the Nile. At the same time, the ruling family of the pharaohs died out. As a result, the question of who was to sit on the throne became a source of conflict between provincial governors. Egypt again split into two kingdoms, each trying to dominate the other. Egypt was left weakened as it faced a new danger from beyond its borders, the Hyksos.

Around 1800 B.C. these mysterious invaders began to sweep across the border into Egypt from Syria and Palestine. The Egyptian armies were no match for them. The invaders brought new weapons that enabled them to easily defeat the Egyptians. While the Egyptians went to war lightly clad and armed with javelins and simple bows, the Hyksos faced them in chain mail and helmets. They also used a composite bow made of wood, horn, and animal tendons that could shoot much farther than the Egyptian bows. Most terrifying of all, the Hyksos rode in a war machine not seen before in Egypt, the horse-drawn chariot.

After burning cities and destroying temples, the Hyksos leaders established themselves as pharaohs. Thus began the period in Egyptian history known as the Second Intermediate Period (1674–1558 B.C.).

An Egyptian pharaoh still ruled in Upper Egypt but was under the control of the Hyksos pharaoh in Lower Egypt. The Hyksos pharaohs ruled wisely. Instead of imposing their own ways, they adapted and borrowed from the Egyptians. Much of the administration remained in Egyptian hands. Hyksos kings also built temples to Egyptian gods, adopted Egyptian hieroglyphics, and copied Middle Kingdom styles of sculpture.

At first the Egyptians and Hyksos lived together without difficulty. Eventually, however, the Egyptian pharaoh in Upper Egypt grew strong enough to challenge the invaders for control of Egypt. They soon discovered that the Hyksos would not leave without a fight.

Discussion

1. How did the Middle Kingdom hope to avoid the problems that brought down the Old Kingdom?
2. Why did the Middle Kingdom collapse?
3. How do you think the Hyksos invasion changed Egyptian society?

Map Activities

Using map A, locate and label the modern states of Djibouti, Ethiopia, Somalia, Yemen, Sudan, Lebanon, and Crete (which belongs to Greece). Also locate and label the modern cities of Khartoum, Asmera, Adan, and Aswan. Also locate and label the Nile River, the Red Sea, the Gulf of Aden, the Arabian Sea, and Lake Faiyum. Finally, using a pen or pencil of a different color, locate and label the ancient city of Byblos just south of modern-day Beirut; Punt, which was probably Somalia; and Nubia, which was southern Egypt.

Name _____ Date _____

CHALLENGES

1. Where was Punt?

_____

2. What did the Egyptians import from Nubia?

_____

_____

3. What did the Egyptians import from Lebanon?

_____

_____

4. Why was clothing so important?

_____

5. What did Egyptian nobles wear?

_____

_____

6. What did Egyptian women use for makeup?

_____

_____

7. How did the Egyptians use Lake Faiyum?

_____

_____

8. What was the most terrifying of all of the new weapons that the invaders used against the Egyptians?

_____

9. What were the invaders called?

_____

10. What is the period after the fall of the Middle Kingdom called?

_____

36

THE WARRIOR PHARAOHS OF THE NEW KINGDOM

The nobleman, Amosis, son of Ebana, was pleased with himself. He had been fighting the Hyksos invaders for several years under the leadership of the pharaoh. He had always been a good soldier. In the siege of Avaris, a Hyksos town, Amosis had carried off one man and three women as prisoners. Because of his courage, the pharaoh awarded him with the gold of valor and his prisoners as slaves. After a three-year siege, the town of Sharuhen finally fell, and once again Amosis carried off two women. Again they were given to him as slaves, and again the pharaoh gave him the gold of valor. The gold enabled Amosis to add to his lands, enlarge his palace, and begin to build and equip his tomb. The slaves supplied much-

The large war chariots of the Hittites carried three soldiers.

needed help to his wife, who managed Amosis's growing household and estates. Now returning from the latest victory of the new pharaoh, Thutmose I, Amosis felt that he had reached the pinnacle of his career as an army officer. During the battle, while the pharaoh watched, Amosis had been able to capture a chariot, its horse, and its charioteer. The chariot had been one of the secret weapons that had enabled the Hyksos to overrun Egypt years before. Now, however, the Egyptians used them and were driving the Hyksos beyond the border. Amosis gleefully anticipated more rewards for his latest capture.

After Egyptians like Amosis defeated and expelled the Hyksos, the pharaoh began to put the new weapons like the chariot and the composite bow to use in conquering an empire. For the first time in Egyptian history, the pharaoh had a professional standing army. A career in the army became a way for men of talent to move up the ladder of success. In the Old and Middle Kingdoms, only noblemen could hold high office. In the New Kingdom, men like Amenhotep-son-of-Hapu, who started life as a simple scribe in the army, could work their way up to be the pharaoh's chief advisors. Amenhotep-son-of-Hapu was eventually worshipped as a god.

The term historians use to describe this period of warlike expansion is the New Kingdom (1558–1085 B.C.). Under Thutmose III, the Egyptian Empire spread into Syria and Palestine, where Egyptian armies clashed with rival empires for control of the Middle East. Thutmose III fought 17 military campaigns during his reign. To administer his empire he brought nobles from the conquered territories to Egypt where he educated and trained them. Then they returned to their homelands and governed them as loyal servants of the pharaoh. The chief rivals of the Egyptians were the Hittites. The two empires faced off in the epic battle

37

of Kadesh. Here 2,500 Hittite chariots of King Muwatalli clashed with a smaller number of Egyptian chariots led by Ramses II. The large three-man chariots of the Hittites easily drove the light two-man Egyptian chariots before them. For a time, it seemed that the Egyptian army would be routed and all would be lost. Ramses found himself surrounded by enemy chariots. In desperation, he prayed to the god Amon-Re and reminded him of all the temples he had built in his honor. The Hittites eventually broke off the battle to raid the Egyptian camp. When they did, the Egyptians counter-attacked and scattered the Hittite army. Many more years of warfare followed before the two sides finally decided upon peace. To finalize the agreement, Ramses even married a Hittite princess.

The New Kingdom pharaohs were also great builders. Ramses II, the greatest of the builders, ordered the huge temple of Abu Simbel to be cut from the rock of a cliff overlooking the Nile. The Egyptians removed an estimated 365,000 tons of rock to create the structure. It was designed in such a way that on two mornings each year, 30 days before the spring equinox and 30 days after the autumnal equinox, the Sun's rays could penetrate the 200 feet of darkness to light up the statues deep in the temple's interior. On either side of the doorway, four 67-foot statues of a seated Ramses were to guard the entrance. In the 1960s this temple, along with others, was threatened by the construction of the Aswan High Dam, which was intended to control the flooding of the Nile and give the modern Egyptians hydro-electric power. To save it for future generations, an international team of engineers cut the gigantic temple into blocks and moved it 200 feet above the original site.

Ramses II also made Thebes into an impressive monumental capital city. He expanded the already huge temple to Amon-Re at Karnak to an area that covers 6,000 square yards. It is big enough to accommodate the entire cathedral of Notre Dame. It was probably the largest religious structure ever built and ranks as one of the seven wonders of the ancient world.

Discussion

1. How did the New Kingdom differ from the Middle Kingdom?
2. Why do you think that New Kingdom pharaohs decided to create an empire?
3. What weaknesses do you see in the New Kingdom?

Map Activities

Using map D, locate and label the modern states of Egypt, Syria, Lebanon, Jordan, and Israel. Also locate and label the cities of Cairo, Amman, Beirut, Jerusalem, and Damascus. Also locate and label the Sinai, the Gulf of Suez, the Gulf of Aqaba, and the Mediterranean Sea. Finally, using a pen or pencil of a different color, locate and label the ancient Hyksos city of Avaris, which was located northeast of the modern city of Zagazig; the ancient Hyksos city of Sharuhen just south of the modern city of Gaza; Palestine, which included modern-day Israel and the area west of the Jordan River now owned by Jordan; the battle of Kadesh just southwest of the modern city of Hims in Syria; Abu Simbel, which is just across the Egyptian border from Sudan on the west side of the Nile River; and Karnak, which is near the modern-day city of Luxor.

Name _____ Date _____

CHALLENGES

1. What awards did the pharaoh give to Amosis for his success in battle?

_____

_____

2. Whom did the New Kingdom drive from Egypt?

_____

3. What new weapon did the New Kingdom use to drive out the invaders?

_____

4. What areas did the New Kingdom conquer?

_____

5. Who were the Egyptians' main rivals for power in the Middle East?

_____

6. Where did the two rival powers clash?

_____

7. What advantage did the Hittites have over the Egyptians in battle?

_____

_____

8. In addition to war, for what were the New Kingdom pharaohs known?

_____

9. What temple was moved to higher ground in the 1960s?

_____

10. Why was the temple moved?

_____

_____

QUEEN HATSHEPSUT: THE WOMAN WHO WAS PHARAOH

Because Egyptian pharaohs were considered divine, it was important for them to find divine wives. Since the only other divine beings in Egypt were in the royal family, pharaohs often married their sisters. One such sister and wife of a pharaoh was Hatshepsut. She, however, broke with tradition when her husband died and ruled as pharaoh in the place of her son, Thutmose III. She took on the official title "she who embraces Amun, the foremost of women."

Throughout Egyptian history, many of the pharaohs' queens wielded equal power with their husbands, but none had been able to seize the throne and become pharaoh themselves. Not only was she the first woman to become pharaoh, but she was also the most successful until Cleopatra 1,400 years later. As is true for most of the New Kingdom pharaohs, she could

This sphinx of Hatshepsut depicts her wearing the ceremonial false beard of the pharaohs.

be warlike. She led Egyptian armies in person against Nubia in the south.

Hatshepsut is better known for her building program that included a huge and beautiful terraced mortuary temple at Deir-el-Bahri. Unlike most temples, it is open to the Sun so that a visitor can study the 190 statues and carvings in the full light of day. The mummy, however, was not to rest here. Aware of the fact that the tombs of the Old and Middle Kingdoms had almost all been robbed, Hatshepsut, like the rest of the New Kingdom pharaohs, had a hidden tomb cut in the rock of the Valley of the Kings. Her tomb features a long corridor that ends in a large burial chamber. Like the above-ground tombs of the previous kingdoms, the walls were decorated with inscriptions and scenes of the afterlife painted in brilliant colors. Here, it was hoped, the mummy, surrounded by unbelievable amounts of riches, would be hidden forever.

The architect of this beautiful temple was Hatshepsut's trusted assistant, Senmut. In order to get himself a share of the queen's eternal life, he secretly sneaked carvings of his own image onto some unobtrusive walls of the temple. When Hatshepsut discovered what he had done, she ordered wreckers to destroy his tomb and deface most of the hidden images that he had placed in her temple.

Hatshepsut is also famous for restoring Egypt to its former wealth by renewing foreign commerce. For example, in the ninth year of her reign, she sent five large cargo ships on a trading expedition to the land of Punt. Modern historians believe that Punt may have been where modern Somalia is now. According to the pictures that decorate her mortuary temple, the expedition was met by the local prince and his wife. After a great feast, the Egyptian captains began to trade for the many wonders of Punt. They loaded their ships with

40

myrrh trees used for incense, beautiful black ebony wood, ivory, gold, and eye cosmetics. The Egyptians were also interested in the many exotic animals found in Punt. On the return journey, one of the Egyptian ships must have looked like Noah's Ark. On it the Egyptians loaded giraffes, hippopotami, apes, monkeys, and greyhounds.

Hatshepsut proved to be an able ruler for 20 years. By avoiding war where she could, she gave Egypt a breathing space in which it could recover its strength. Yet her position on the throne was not secure. As a woman, Egyptian law said that she technically could not rule as pharaoh. She tried to encourage her people to believe that she was a legitimate pharaoh by disguising her gender. She adopted the ceremonial false beard and masculine dress of male pharaohs. In some of her inscriptions she even calls herself "His Majesty." As Thutmose III, who had been declared pharaoh before Hatshepsut seized the throne, grew into manhood, his impatience and resentment toward the strong-willed woman increased. Finally, he gathered the supporters that he needed and overthrew the queen. We do not know the details of this event, but it is likely that Hatshepsut was killed as a result.

Thutmose III tried to undo all that his mother had accomplished. He abandoned peaceful relations with neighboring countries and launched attacks into Nubia and Palestine. He also destroyed Hatshepsut's statues and erased her name from all the temples and monuments that she had constructed during her reign.

Discussion

1. How did Hatshepsut try to make herself acceptable as pharaoh?
2. What conclusions can you draw about Hatshepsut's personality?
3. How did Hatshepsut strengthen the power of the Middle Kingdom?

Map Activities

Using map D, locate and label the modern states of Egypt, Sudan, Libya, Jordan, and Israel. Also locate and label the cities of Aswan, Luxor, Asyut, and Cairo. Locate and label the Nile River, the Jordan River, the Red Sea, and the Eastern desert. Finally, using a pen or pencil of a different color, locate and label ancient Nubia, which was the area south of modern Aswan; the Valley of the Kings, which is just across the river and north of the modern city of Luxor; and the Mortuary Temple of Deir-el-Bahri, which is located immediately south of the Valley of the Kings.

Name _____ Date _____

CHALLENGES

1. Who was the son of Hatshepsut?

_____

2. How did Hatshepsut break with tradition?

_____

3. What is remarkable about Deir-el-Bahri?

_____

4. How did Hatshepsut try to keep grave robbers from her tomb?

_____

_____

5. Who designed Hatshepsut's temple?

_____

6. Why did Hatshepsut deface his tomb?

_____

7. How did Hatshepsut help to restore Egypt to its former wealth?

_____

_____

8. What did the trading expedition to Punt bring back?

_____

_____

9. How long did Hatshepsut rule?

_____

10. Why was her position as pharaoh insecure?

_____

_____

42

AKHENATON THE BIZARRE

One of the most extraordinary and mysterious pharaohs in Egyptian history is Amenhotep IV. His statues show a grotesque figure with a huge, narrow head perched on top of a very long, thin neck, a potbelly like a pregnant woman, along with womanly hips, all somehow held up by tiny slender shins. Archaeologists have come up with many possible explanations for Amenhotep's remarkable physical characteristics. Some say that he suffered from a glandular disorder that deformed his body. Others say that he wanted to emphasize his closeness with a creator god, so he had himself portrayed with both male and female characteristics.

Early in his reign he clashed with the powerful priests of the god Amon-Re. He was often known as the king of the gods and was portrayed with many differ-

Pharaoh Akhenaton and his wife Nefertiti are shown giving offerings to the sun disk Aton. Note Akhenaton's unusual figure.

ent forms. Amon-Re had become the chief god of the New Kingdom, and his priests had been awarded wealth to rival even the pharaoh. Amenhotep IV was determined to restore the power of the pharaoh. He reacted to the Amon-Re priests by forbidding worship of their god and erasing his name from monuments. Amenhotep IV replaced Amon-Re with a different god called Aton, the solar disk. The pharaoh even changed his name from Amenhotep, which honored Amon-Re, to Akhenaton, which meant "pleasant to Aton."

Historians refer to Akhenaton's reign as the Amarna period. It is named after the pharaoh's new city located at Amarna on the edge of the desert. The new city saw fascinating times. By piecing together surviving fragments of literature and sculpture from the period, archaeologists have come to believe that Akhenaton was motivated by more than just jealousy of the priests of Amon-Re. The fragments show an intense devotion to Aton as a benevolent god of all nations, not just Egypt. Worship of all other gods was discouraged. Because of this Akhenaton is often called the first *monotheist* in history. A monotheist is someone who worships only one god. In fact, it was more complicated than that. Akhenaton himself was worshipped as a god, and the Egyptian people could only worship Aton through the pharaoh.

The Amarna period is also known for more realistic art forms than before. Graffiti by Akhenaton's chief sculptor, Bek, says that it was the pharaoh himself who taught the artists the new way of looking at life. As we have already noted, Akhenaton's distinctive human characteristics are portrayed in his portraits. In other ways Egyptian artists for the first time tried to create more natural and life-like images. Artists painted ordinary scenes of plants and animals seen along the Nile. Akhenaton ordered the court sculptors to break with tradition on how they portrayed the pharaoh. Instead of the expressionless and remote, god-like image of earlier pharaohs, Akhenaton is often shown with his wife, Nefertiti, and their children. In one relief sculpture, Akhenaton is shown kissing one of his daughters, while the other two play in the lap of their mother. Also, a famous, life-like portrait bust of Nefertiti survives that shows a beautiful woman whose makeup and hairstyle would make her look at home in any modern woman's fashion magazine.

The writings of the time also show a new creativity. Akhenaton introduced everyday language and idiomatic expressions into literature. Egyptian poets experimented with new expressions and ideas.

Despite Akhenaton's efforts, he ultimately failed. His veneration of Aton did not survive him. When he died, the priests of Amon-Re quickly re-established control. The name of Akhenaton and his god Aton were hammered out. His city was abandoned to the desert. Also, so distracted was he by his religious reforms that he ignored the pleas for help from his borders. Enemy Hittite warriors overran the Egyptian possessions in Syria and Palestine. During his reign local government was allowed to become corrupt. Seizures of lands belonging to the priests of Amon-Re disrupted the economy. Finally, the construction of the new capital left an exhausted treasury. To the next pharaoh, Akhenaton left a very weakened and confused Egypt.

Discussion

1. Why would Amenhotep IV feel that he had to create a new religion to take power away from the priests of Amon-Re?
2. How did Aton differ from other Egyptian gods?
3. Why do you think Amenhotep IV instructed his artists to be more realistic?

Map Activities

Using map D, locate and label the modern states of Egypt, Sudan, Libya, Lebanon, and Israel. Also locate and label the cities of Tel Aviv, Elat, and Suez. Also locate and label the Nile River, the Red Sea, and modern Lake Nasser. Finally, using a pen or pencil of a different color, locate and label the ancient capital of Amarna, which was just across the Nile from the modern city of Deir Mawas; and label Palestine, which is made up of modern Israel and the area to the west of the Jordan River owned by Jordan.

Name _____ Date _____

CHALLENGES

1. How do archaeologists explain Amenhotep IV's strange shape?

_____

_____

2. Who seemed to be Amenhotep IV's chief enemies?

_____

3. Why was he jealous of them?

_____

_____

4. What was the name of Amenhotep IV's new god?

_____

5. What was Amenhotep IV's new name?

_____

6. What do historians call the reign of Amenhotep?

_____

7. What was distinctive about this new period?

_____

_____

8. Who was Nefertiti?

_____

9. What happened when Amenhotep IV died?

_____

_____

10. What happened while Amenhotep IV was distracted with religious reform?

_____

_____

THE TOMB OF TUTANKHAMEN

Archaeologist Howard Carter had been digging in the Valley of the Kings for six long years. During that time, he and his Egyptian workers had sifted through mounds of rubble, dug endless trenches, and moved huge quantities of dirt. Other archaeologists believed he was a fool to think that he could find the tomb of Tutankhamen. In time, he too began to doubt that he would ever find the lost tomb. This day looked as if it would be like all the others, he thought, as he trudged down into the dusty valley in the early morning glare. Yet this was not to be a day like all the rest. After several hours of the usual hard work, he was surprised to hear shouts coming from the Egyptian workers. He ran down to see what had happened and stopped dead in his tracks. Before him lay the stone steps of a tomb just

The innermost coffin that held Tutankhamen's body was made of solid gold and weighed over a ton.

unearthed. After several more hours of clearing away soil, the door of the tomb was opened. A rush of dry, cold, ancient air met his face. When he cast his lamp into the darkness ahead, he beheld strange animals, breathtaking statues, and the glint of gold everywhere. At last he had found Tutankhamen's tomb.

Unlike the rest of the New Kingdom pharaohs, Tutankhamen's tomb eluded grave robbers, leaving it almost intact to be discovered by Carter in 1922. It remains as probably the world's most exciting archaeological discovery. It took Carter eight years to remove, catalog, and restore the more than 2,000 objects found in the tomb. The amount of wealth buried with the pharaoh was almost unbelievable. Yet Tutankhamen was a lesser pharaoh and would probably be almost unknown if not for the discovery of his tomb.

Upon Akhenaton's death, Egypt was thrown into turmoil for a few years. Finally, order was partially restored when Akhenaton's ten-year-old son-in-law was crowned pharaoh. He took the name Tutankhamen. Under the new king, the priests of Amon-Re re-established their authority. The worship of Aton was abolished and Akhenaton's city was abandoned. The temples to Aton were dismantled and the materials shipped across the river to build new temples to Amon-Re. The power of the Amon-Re priesthood was never again challenged. Tutankhamen's reign lasted only nine years, and he was buried, like the rest of the New Kingdom pharaohs, in the Valley of the Kings. The mummy of Tutankhamen reveals that he probably died from a blow to his head. In any case, his death was premature because he left no heirs. His widow, Ankhesenamun, desperately tried to maintain order by finding another husband. She appealed to the Hittite king Suppiluliumas to send one of his sons to marry her and become pharaoh. The Hittite prince made it only as far as the Egyptian border where he was mysteriously murdered. Ankhesenamun apparently lost control and a period of instability followed. Eventually, a new dynasty was established when a military commander named Ramses II seized the throne.

Tutankhamen's tomb reveals how a little-known pharaoh was equipped to enter the next world. How much more wealthy must have been the tombs of the greater pharaohs who followed Tutankhamen on the throne! These men oversaw the final glorious years of Egyptian civilization. Seti I launched military campaigns into Palestine and Syria to win back provinces lost during Akhenaton's reign. Ramses II completed the largest Egyptian temple ever built at Karnak, which covered 6,000 square yards. Ramses III successfully fought off a dangerous invasion of the so-called Sea Peoples, whom historians believe were probably early Greeks.

By the end of Ramses III's reign, however, Egypt was in decline. The costs of maintaining a huge army, building monumental temples, and keeping the priests of Amon-Re content were draining the pharaoh's treasury. Grave robbing had become so bad that a number of mummies from the Valley of the Kings had been removed and placed in a common tomb where they could be better guarded. After the death of Ramses III, eight more pharaohs ruled with the name Ramses as Egypt slid into chaos. Finally, a succession of foreign invaders swept into Egypt and battled amongst themselves for control. The Libyans were overthrown by the Nubians, who themselves were overthrown by the Assyrians. Egypt, the home of an ancient and magnificent civilization, by the eighth century B.C. was merely a province of somebody else's empire.

Discussion

1. What do you think were the characteristics of Tutankhamen's reign?
2. What does Tutankhamen's tomb tell us about New Kingdom pharaohs?
3. Why would foreigners want to invade New Kingdom Egypt?

Map Activities

Using map D, locate and label the modern states of Egypt, Syria, Libya, Jordan, and Israel. Also locate and label the cities of Jerusalem, Beirut, Gaza, Alexandria, and Cairo. Locate and label the Nile River, the Jordan River, the Red Sea, the Gulf of Aqaba, and the Gulf of Suez. Finally, using a pen or pencil of a different color, locate and label the ancient capital of Amarna, which was just across the Nile from the modern city of Deir Mawas; the Valley of the Kings, which is located across the river and north of the modern city of Luxor; Karnak, which is north of Luxor on the same side of the river; and Palestine, which is made up of modern Israel and the area to the west of the Jordan River owned by Jordan.

Name _____ Date _____

CHALLENGES

1. Where was Tutankhamen's tomb?

_____

2. When was the tomb discovered and by whom?

_____

3. What was so remarkable about Tutankhamen's tomb compared to other pharaohs?

_____

4. How long was Tutankhamen pharaoh?

_____

5. How did the priests of Amon-Re undo the reforms of Akhenaton?

_____

_____

6. What were the accomplishments of Seti I?

_____

_____

7. What did Ramses II accomplish?

_____

_____

8. Why did Egypt decline?

_____

_____

9. When did the New Kingdom begin to decline?

_____

10. Who were the foreign invaders who occupied Egypt?

_____

_____

THE RISE AND FALL OF EMPIRES IN THE MIDDLE EAST

Suppiliuma stroked his chin. "These may be the horses that I seek," he said to his servant. They looked strong and sure-footed. They had been specially bred to draw the large Hittite war chariots. Unlike other nations, the Hittites mounted three heavily-armed men instead of two. To pull such a load at high speed into battle, the Hittites learned to be master horsemen. There was even a detailed Hittite manual on horse care: when to wash them, rub them with oil, care for their feet. As a Hittite warrior, the most important things in Suppiliuma's life were his horses and his chariot.

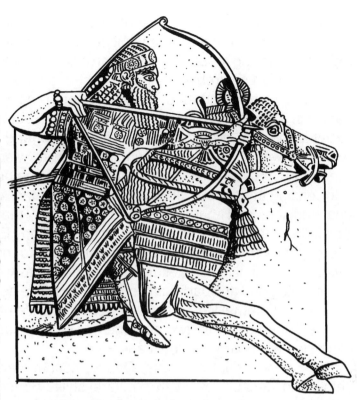

King Assurbanipal of Assyria ruled over an empire that stretched from Egypt to Iran.

With their mighty chariots, the Hittites conquered most of the Middle East, except for Egypt. The Hittites were more than just horsemen and conquerors, however. They borrowed cuneiform writing from the Babylonians to keep detailed records and preserve hymns and myths. They also built a beautiful capital city at Hattusa in Anatolia, which is part of modern-day Turkey. Hattusa was surrounded by walls 25 feet thick. Every 100 feet, square, double towers guarded gateways into the city. Within Hittite palaces, the walls were decorated with images of Hittites fighting battles and celebrating festivals. They depicted themselves as short and stocky with high cheekbones and recessed chins. From Hattusa the Hittite kings administered their empire through a surprisingly humane law code. Instead of following the old Babylonian law codes that required an eye for an eye, the Hittite laws were based on restitution. Arsonists were required to replace property that they set afire. Murderers could go free after they paid the family of the victim a large amount of silver, slaves, or land. Hittite society was feudal. Nobles held land from the king in return for promises of troops and chariots in time of war. Yet, after only 500 years, Hattusa was attacked by the mysterious Sea Peoples and destroyed along with most of its population.

The Middle East wasn't to be without an empire for long. The Assyrian Empire stepped into the space once filled by the Hittites. They came from the northern part of Mesopotamia. Their empire, however, was far different. Their chief deity was Ashur, the god of war. As a result, they were interested only in preserving tradition and the arts and sciences of armed conflict. Instead of law codes, the Assyrians relied on terror and intimidation to control the Middle East. The Assyrian king Shalmaneser I behaved like a typical Assyrian king when he blinded 14,000 defeated enemy soldiers and then carried them off to Assyria as slaves. The Assyrians also forced conquered peoples to move from their homes to new

     49

lands where they were used as forced labor to build impressive cities like the capital, Nineveh. However, such actions ultimately failed, and the Assyrian kings spent much of their time crushing rebellions. At last, an alliance, including many of those who had suffered under Assyrian control, rose up and destroyed the empire.

The last and greatest Middle Eastern empire of the ancient world was that of the Persians. Their home was in modern-day Iran, but their empire stretched from the Indus Valley across the Middle East to include Egypt and the Ionian coast. The Persian kings, beginning with their founder Cyrus, ruled with wisdom and toleration. Unlike Egyptian pharaohs, Cyrus left instructions for his body to be buried in a small, simple tomb. Instead of terrorizing the people within their empire like the Assyrians did, the Persians respected local traditions and honored the local gods. They tried to interfere as little as possible with the affairs of the people within their empire, be they Egyptian, Mesopotamian, or Assyrian. The origin of this attitude can be seen in the founder of their religion, Zoroaster. This mysterious man lived sometime in the sixth century B.C. and taught that the universe was divided into good and bad, light and darkness. The god of light was Ahura Mazda. To follow him and find eternal life, one must lead a moral life based on truth. Although the empire of the Persians fell within two centuries of its foundation, there are still those who follow Zoroaster in modern-day India and Iran.

A descendant of Cyrus, Darius, constructed a great capital at Persepolis. The Persian builders borrowed architectural styles from all over the Middle East. The city was built on terraces like Babylon. Its walls were decorated with reliefs of Assyrian human-headed bulls. The doorways looked like those found in Egyptian temples. Finally, columns from far-off Greece held up the roof of the audience hall. At the time, Darius would never have dreamt that the Greeks would someday come to dominate the political and cultural life of Persia.

Discussion

1. Compare and contrast the Persian Empire with the Assyrian Empire.
2. How did the Hittite law code differ from the Babylonian?
3. Why did the Middle East go through a period of one empire after another?
4. How might the Persian Empire have been a reaction to the Assyrian Empire?

Map Activities

Using map A, locate and label the modern states of Iran, Iraq, Turkey, Syria, Georgia, Armenia, and Azerbaijan. Also locate and label the Tigris and Euphrates Rivers and the area called Kurdistan that runs across southern Turkey, northern Iraq, and into Iran. Finally, using a pen or pencil of a different color, locate and label the ancient city of Hattusa, which was located about 30 miles northeast of the modern Turkish city of Kirikkale; Babylonia, which is the area between the Tigris and Euphrates Rivers in the south; the ancient city of Nineveh, which was located just north of the modern Iraqi city of Mosul; Ionia, which was the southwestern coast of Turkey; and Persepolis, which was near the modern Iranian city of Shiraz.

Name _____ Date _____

CHALLENGES

1. Why did the Hittites need to be master horsemen?

_____

_____

2. What evidence is there that the Hittites took their horsemanship seriously?

_____

_____

3. What was the extent of the Hittite Empire?

_____

4. Where was the Hittite capital?

_____

5. What is remarkable about the Hittites?

_____

6. How did the Assyrians maintain control of their empire?

_____

_____

7. Where was the Assyrian capital?

_____

8. What was the last and greatest of the Middle Eastern empires?

_____

9. Who was their greatest leader?

_____

10. According to Zoroaster, how did you find eternal life?

_____

_____

THE CREATIVE NATIONS OF PHOENICIA AND ISRAEL

The ship was deep in fog. Those sailors who steered the ship from the stern could just barely make out the bow. The air was heavy and the only sound that could be heard was the splash of the oars as the vessel moved forward into the gray morning. It had been almost a year since these Phoenician sailors had raised anchor and sailed from the port of Tyre, leaving the snow-covered Lebanon Mountains behind them. Their voyage had taken them first to Egypt, where they traded cedar logs for Egyptian cloth. From there they sailed along the coast of North Africa for many days until they landed at the thriving Phoenician colony of Carthage. Here they took on fresh supplies and bronze armor, carved ivory, and purple cloth to trade. Again they set sail, passing through the Strait of Gibraltar and heading north along the coast of

Phoenician ships carried the traders from Lebanon, throughout the Mediterranean, and all the way to Britain.

Spain using the North Star for navigation at night. After many days of hugging the sparsely populated coast of Europe, they at last steered for the remote island of Britain. As the morning sun gradually cleared away the fog, the sailors could see the high, white cliffs of the coast of Britain.

The Phoenicians were the first great navigators of the Middle East. Because their narrow land, which today is called Lebanon, is trapped between the mountains and the sea, the Phoenicians found that the best way to survive was by going to sea and becoming traders. They developed solid ocean-going vessels that rode the Mediterranean when it turned stormy, yet could carry in their holds cargo to be traded throughout the Middle East, North Africa, and the coasts of Europe. They also learned to navigate these ships by the stars.

The cedars of Lebanon were prized by other nations like the Egyptians for building ships, but the most profitable trade was cloth dyed by phoinix. Phoinix was a dye extracted from shellfish that the Phoenicians used to color cloth a deep purple. Because the Phoenicians could demand a high price, only kings could afford it. It is for this reason that purple became the color of royalty.

The Phoenicians left other legacies. In order to make trade easier, they came up with a simple alphabet of 22 symbols. In modified form, this later became the alphabet that you're reading right now. The Phoenicians also left colonies all over the Mediterranean that later turned into important cities like Palermo, Cadiz, and Carthage. Finally, they spread the knowledge of weaving, glass-making, and metallurgy developed by their neighbors in the Middle East throughout the ancient world.

Another small nation that had a large impact was that of the Hebrews. We know a great deal about the history of the Hebrews because it makes up much of the first half of the

Bible, known to Christians as the Old Testament. The Hebrews are remarkable because they developed a *monotheistic* religion. Monotheism is a belief in one god. Central to their religion was the belief that they had a covenant with God, whom they called Yahweh or Jehovah. They believed that they were to worship and be obedient to him alone and that in return, he would bring blessings to them. On the other hand, if the Hebrews were disobedient, they would be punished. As a result, the Hebrews took history very seriously as the way to understand God's actions.

At first the Hebrews were wandering nomads, but eventually they were enslaved in Egypt. Under the guidance of Moses, they fled into Sinai. After many years they at last entered the promised land of Palestine. There they defeated the local population, called the Canaanites. For two centuries their kingdom thrived. Under king Solomon they enjoyed a golden age. Solomon acquired cedar logs from the Phoenicians and built a huge temple for Yahweh at Jerusalem. He also built a magnificent palace for himself and powerful fortresses to defend the realm.

When Solomon died, however, the Hebrews split into separate kingdoms, called Israel and Judah. They were not to be independent for long. In 722 B.C. the Assyrians captured much of Israel, and a century and a half later, Jerusalem (the capital of Judah) itself was destroyed by the Chaldeans. Many Hebrews were marched off to Babylonia. From this point on, the Hebrews were known as Jews.

In exile, the bonds of kinship were strengthened. When they were, at last, allowed to return to their homeland and rebuild the temple at Jerusalem, they had become a tight-knit community that stressed law, ritual, and tradition. Later, the Jews were to be exiled from their homeland again, but they preserved their traditions in two important collections of books. These are called the Talmud, or instructions, and the Torah, which recorded the early history and laws of the Jewish people.

Discussion

1. How did the Phoenicians help to spread Middle Eastern civilization?
2. Why did the Hebrews stress the bonds of kinship?
3. Compare and contrast the Hebrews with the Phoenicians.
4. What legacies have both left to the modern world?

Map Activities

Using map C, locate and label the modern states of Spain, Tunisia, Algeria, Morocco, Great Britain, and Lebanon. Also locate and label the Strait of Gibraltar. Using a pen or pencil of a different color, locate and label the ancient city of Carthage, which was very near to modern-day Tunis, and the ancient city of Tyre, which still exists in modern Lebanon. Trace the route of the Phoenician sailors described in the reading that took them from Tyre to Britain.

Using map B, locate and label the modern states of Israel, Syria, Iraq, Jordan, Lebanon, and Egypt. Also locate and label the Sinai Peninsula, the Jordan River, and the Mediterranean Sea. Finally, using a pen or pencil of a different color, locate and label the ancient kingdom of Judah, which included the area in modern Israel from Jerusalem south, and the kingdom of Israel, which included the area of modern Israel north of Jerusalem.

Name _____ Date _____

CHALLENGES

1. Why did the Phoenicians turn to trade?

_____

_____

2. What advantages did Phoenician ships enjoy?

_____

_____

3. Where did the Phoenicians trade?

_____

_____

4. What was the most profitable Phoenician product?

_____

5. What did the Phoenicians invent to make trade easier?

_____

6. Why are the Hebrews remarkable?

_____

_____

7. Why did the Hebrews take history very seriously?

_____

8. What were the names of the two Hebrew kingdoms?

_____

9. For what building projects is Solomon known?

_____

10. When did the Hebrews become known as Jews?

_____

ALEXANDER THE GREAT CONQUERS HIS WORLD

Alexander the Great

Alexander stood pondering the huge intricate bundle of ancient rope. This was the famous Gordian Knot. Legend said that he who could untie the Gordian Knot would be lord of all Asia. Some months before, Alexander had raised a huge army of Greeks and Macedonians and set out to conquer the Persian Empire. The route of his campaign had already taken him along the Ionian coast where he freed the Greek cities that had fallen under Persian control. Already, he could boast of one victory won over the Persians at the Granicus River, though it had been a close battle. In the midst of the fighting, a Persian commander struck Alexander with a battle axe. The axe shattered his helmet, but almost miraculously he survived. Alexander took this as a good sign that he would succeed. Now, as he stood before the Gordian Knot, he pulled out his sword and slashed at the knot until it was cut. Hence, all the world would know that it was Alexander the Great who would fulfill the prophesy.

Before setting off on his conquests, Alexander had inherited the powerful kingdom of Macedonia from his father, Philip. Macedonia had been a mountainous and backward kingdom on the far northern border of Greece. Although they spoke a language similar to the Greeks of Athens in the south, they did not share in the great outburst of Greek civilization. They looked on while the Athenians created spectacular architecture, conducted advanced scientific experiments, developed profound philosophy, and created some of the most beautiful art and literature the world has ever enjoyed.

Under Philip's leadership, Macedonia began to absorb much of this advanced Greek civilization. Greece, however, was not a single state but many warring city-states. Philip took advantage of these divisions to bring most of Greece under his control. Having achieved this, he decided to attack Persia, but before he could launch his attack, he was assassinated. Unfortunately for the Persians, Alexander was no ordinary 20-year-old when he inherited the throne of Macedonia. He was not only determined to carry on what his father had begun, but he also wanted to unite the known world under his power.

After cutting the Gordian Knot, Alexander marched toward Phoenicia where he hoped to capture the ports used by the Persian fleet. He captured Byblos and Sidon easily, but the island city of Tyre still held out. Alexander had to build a causeway of stones as a bridge for his men to attack the city, and in the end Tyre fell. The Persian fleet was dispersed because it no longer had a harbor. Next, Alexander conquered Egypt and founded a new city called Alexandria. This became the most important city in Alexander's empire. From his new city, Alexander traveled across the Libyan desert to consult the priest of the Egyptian god Amon-Re at Ammonium. There Alexander was himself addressed as a god. Content with this reception, he set out once again with his army, this time for Mesopotamia.

At Gaugamela, the Persian emperor, Darius, decided to make his last stand. The fight was long and bloody, but once again the Macedonians were victorious. Darius fled from the battle but was murdered by one of his own men. With Darius gone, Alexander was declared to be the new Persian emperor. Even with the whole Middle East at his feet, Alexander was not yet satisfied. He wanted to journey to the ends of the earth. After capturing the two capitals of Persia, Susa and Persepolis, Alexander followed the Kabul River downstream to the sacred river of India, the Indus. Here, he met and defeated the war elephants of Porus, the king of the Punjab. Near the site of the battle, Alexander founded a new city named after his horse, Bucephaus, who had been with him since the beginning of his conquests.

By this time, however, Alexander's men were weary of their conquests and were homesick. Alexander pleaded with them to go on, but they refused. After sulking in his tent for three days, Alexander at last began the long journey back by heading south down the Indus River until he reached the Arabian Sea, then west to Persepolis and Susa. The journey was incredibly difficult, and three-quarters of his men perished along the way because of exhaustion and lack of water.

At last he arrived in Susa. Here, to symbolize the union of the Greek and Middle Eastern parts of his empire, he presided over a mass wedding. Eighty of his officers married eighty Persian women. Alexander himself married Barsine, the daughter of Darius. He had great dreams to explore new lands and create a world empire that would unite all people as brothers. He was not to achieve any more of his dreams, however. He traveled to Babylonia to supervise the building of a new temple and make plans to explore the Caspian Sea. While there, he fell ill with fever and died. He was 33 years old.

Alexander's empire did not last long. Soon his generals were fighting among themselves for control. Nevertheless, he had a profound influence on the Middle East. He left an exciting new civilization that mixed ideas from Greece with the dramatically different approaches to life that he found from Egypt to India. This civilization is called Hellenistic. The 300 years after the death of Alexander when the new civilization flourished is called the Hellenistic era. Because it was a time of great toleration and open-mindedness when different cultures could freely mix, there were many great achievements in art, philosophy, and science. The cultural environment also opened up opportunities for new trade between lands very far and different from each other like Greece and India. Yet, the Hellenistic age was also one of violence as various kings, though sharing the new cosmopolitan or international culture, battled to be Alexander's successor and dominate the known world.

Discussion

1. Why was the Hellenistic age a time of toleration and open-mindedness?
2. How was Alexander the Great a good influence on the Middle East? How was he a bad influence?
3. Why did Alexander's empire not survive him?
4. Alexander's visits to the Gordian Knot and the priest of Amon-Re tells you what about his personality?

Name _____ Date _____

CHALLENGES

1. What was the prophecy of the Gordian Knot? _____
_____

2. How did Alexander untie the Gordian Knot? _____
_____

3. How did Philip come to control Greece? _____
_____

4. How old was Alexander when he set out to conquer the world? _____

5. How did Alexander capture Tyre? _____
_____

_____

6. What was the most important city in Alexander's empire? _____

7. How did Alexander try to symbolize the union of the Greek and Middle Eastern civilizations?

_____

8. How old was Alexander when he died? _____

9. What is Hellenistic culture? _____
_____

10. What happened to Alexander's empire after he died?_____
_____

Map Activities

Using map A, locate and label the modern states of Egypt, Jordan, Iraq, Greece, Macedonia, Turkey, Syria, Iran, Afghanistan, and Pakistan. Also locate and label the Granicus River in northwestern Turkey, the Kabul River in the north of modern Afghanistan, the Caspian Sea, and modern Athens in Greece. Finally, using a pen or pencil of a different color, locate and label ancient Persia, which is present day Iran; the ancient Phoenician city of Tyre; the ancient Ammonium near modern el Wahat or Siwa on the western border of Egypt; ancient Gordian near the modern Turkish city of Polatli; Gaugalmela near the modern Iraqi city of Mosul; Persepolis near the modern Iranian city of Shiraz; Susa near the modern Iranian city of Dezful; and the ancient city of Babylon located on the eastern side of the Euphrates River near the modern Iraqi city of Al Hillah. Once you have located these places, use the text to trace as best you can the route followed by Alexander the Great.

THE MIDDLE EAST AND THE ROMAN EMPIRE

The Egyptian warships of Antony and Cleopatra's fleet hovered off the coast of Actium. The day was cool with a soft breeze gently rustling the sails. Suddenly, the watchman on the mast cried out. The dark mass of the Roman fleet emerged like a long snake from behind the headland of the shore. Antony ordered his ships into battle formation and prepared to face the enemy. His heart sank, however, when he turned and saw half his ships follow the massive and brightly decorated vessel of Cleopatra as she fled for Egypt. By abandoning her lover at Actium, Cleopatra had also destroyed her own chances to maintain Egyptian indepen-

The Roman fleet at the Battle of Actium

dence. Within a year, Roman forces occupied Egypt, and to avoid capture, Antony and Cleopatra committed suicide. Egypt became just another province of the Roman Empire.

Like Egypt, the other warring kingdoms in the Middle East that succeeded the empire of Alexander the Great were easy prey for the new empire of the Romans. Rome started out as a small village dominated by neighboring powers. However, the Romans were a dutiful, disciplined, and practical people who excelled in the art of government. In time, their abilities enabled them to dominate first Italy and then the whole Mediterranean. From 29 B.C. to A.D. 14, most of the Middle East except for Persia and part of Mesopotamia also came under Roman control. In fact, many of the Hellenistic princes gladly became clients of Rome. The Roman emperors allowed cooperative local kings to keep their thrones. The new empire offered security from attack under Rome's unbeatable armed forces, as well as efficient government and stability. For several centuries the Middle East settled down to enjoy the Pax Romana, or the Roman Peace. The rich Hellenistic culture left behind by Alexander the Great also made it easy for the Middle East to accept Roman domination. The Romans themselves had borrowed much of their culture from Hellenistic Greece. Most Roman art, philosophy, and architecture was copied from the Greeks.

Not all subject people of the Middle East were happy with Roman rule. After Caligula decided to make himself a god, everyone accepted it except the Jews. Their refusal to bow to his statues at Alexandria led to an attack on Jews. Their women were forced to eat pork (a meat that Jewish ceremonial law forbade) and elders were flogged. Jerusalem, center of the Jewish faith, was in turmoil as rivals battled each other for control. The Roman general Titus attacked in A.D. 70, killing thousands. Their temple was destroyed with only the west wall (known as the wailing wall today) remaining. The revolt was over, except for some Jews who refused to surrender.

58

Destruction of the temple meant the end of the priesthood. The temple was gone, but the Jews still had their law and their religion.

At Masada, which held out for three years, the commander realized that it was only a matter of time until they were conquered. Rather than surrender, each man killed his own wife and children; 10 men were chosen to kill the others, and one of the 10 was chosen to kill the other nine. The last defender set fire to the palace and fell on his own sword. Only two old women and five small children who had hidden themselves survived.

Many of the Jews left then, but not all. Those remaining were allowed to keep their religion, although a new council replaced the high priest and the *Sanhedrin* (the supreme court and legislature). In 132, another revolt broke out that lasted over three years. Many of the Jews were killed, sold into slavery, or forced to leave Jerusalem. Many went to Galilee. Eventually, a Jewish ruler called the *ethnarch* was appointed. That seemed to solve the problem, and for 200 years there were no revolts.

The long period of exile from their homeland and persecution is known in Jewish history as the *Diaspora.* The Jews who fled Jerusalem went in many directions: to Europe, North Africa, and the Middle East. A major center for Jews was Baghdad. There, Jewish scholars were trained in academies, and study of the Talmud (Jewish law) continued. A thriving community remained until the Moslems swept into the region in the seventh century. Others moved to Europe where some Jews had already located. After the breakup of the Roman Empire, they came under Christian rule. Some converted to Christianity, but others kept their faith. The most influential Jewish community in Europe was in Spain.

Discussion

1. Why would the people of the Middle East have been glad to be part of the Roman Empire?
2. Why did the Jews rebel against the Roman domination?
3. Compare the Roman Empire with other empires already studied.

Map Activities

Using map B, locate and label the modern states of Egypt, Israel, Jordan, Lebanon, and Syria. Locate and label the Jordan River, the Dead Sea, and the Golan Heights. Also locate and label Jerusalem, Beirut, and Damascus. Finally, using a pen or pencil of a different color, locate and label ancient Palestine, which included the area of modern Israel and the area owned by Jordan located on the west bank of the Jordan River.

Name _____ Date _____

CHALLENGES

1. How did Antony and Cleopatra avoid capture?

_____

2. Why were the Hellenistic kingdoms easy prey for the Romans?

_____

_____

3. What characteristics did the Romans have?

_____

_____

4. Why did some Hellenistic princes want to become a part of the Roman Empire?

_____

_____

5. What was the Pax Romana?

_____

6. What happened to Jerusalem in A.D. 70?

_____

_____

7. How did the defenders of Masada avoid capture?

_____

_____

8. What is the wailing wall?

_____

9. What was the Diaspora?

_____

_____

10. Where was the most influential Jewish community in Europe?

_____

CHRISTIANITY CONQUERS ROME

The Bedouin boy climbed up to a small clearing on the side of the rocky hill. Still, there was no sign of the lost goat. He scrambled over boulders and fallen rocks as he worked his way towards the top. Then he saw it: a small, cave-like opening in the side of the hill. Perhaps the goat had fallen in. He threw a rock into the black opening. He expected to hear the dull thud of the rock hitting the dirt of the cave floor. Instead, he heard the rock smash something inside. Terrified, he ran back down the hill to the village. Later he returned with his friend. Bolstered by the fact that there were now two of them, they worked their way down into the opening. On the floor they found ancient scrolls that had spilled out from the broken clay jar. But that was not all. As they peered farther into

The followers of Jesus, who were called Christians, spread his teachings throughout the Middle East and the Roman Empire.

the cave, they saw more jars looming out of the darkness. These contained what would later come to be known as the Dead Sea Scrolls.

The scrolls belonged to a group of pious Jews called the Essenes. They were one of a number of rival Jewish sects that existed during the second and first century B.C. Like the other groups at that time, they believed that the end of the world was at hand. They looked forward to the arrival of a messiah sent by God to save his people. It was into this environment that Jesus was born probably around 4 B.C. No other documents of the time mention Jesus and his teachings, so historians and religious scholars rely on the first four books of the New Testament, which are called the Gospels. These are the books Matthew, Mark, Luke, and John. From these we learn that Jesus was born to a Jewish family and was educated in the Jewish religion. At about age 30, he began to preach a message of love and forgiveness that minimized the old rituals and laws of the Jews. While some accepted his message, most did not because it differed from conventional Jewish wisdom and practice. Eventually, the authorities in Palestine saw him as a threat to the peace because crowds began to proclaim him as king or Messiah. They feared that the Romans would interpret this as a sign of revolt. They also saw him as a threat to their own power. Jesus was arrested by them and turned over to the Roman governor, Pontius Pilate, who, perhaps somewhat reluctantly, ordered his death by crucifixion.

During the days and weeks after his death, Jesus's followers reported seeing and talking to him. They proclaimed him the Messiah and announced that he would soon return to establish the kingdom of Heaven on Earth. At first, the early followers of Jesus did little to spread his teachings. The man who deserves the most credit for carrying the new faith

61

beyond Palestine and the small segment of Jewish believers was Paul. Before his conversion, he had been well educated. As a result, he had the knowledge and skill to carry the message of Christianity to both gentiles (non-Jews) who were poor and uneducated and those who were well versed in Hellenistic culture. By the time of Paul's death, Christianity had spread throughout the eastern Mediterranean and all the way to Rome.

At first, the Christians suffered persecution at the hands of Roman officials. For example, the Emperor Nero blamed a fire that burned much of Rome on the Christians. He used this as an excuse to arrest, torture, and execute many Christians, including Paul and the apostle Peter (one of twelve men selected by Jesus while he was on Earth to spread his message). Nevertheless, the religion continued to thrive and many people were converted throughout the Middle East and North Africa. Eventually, the Roman emperors themselves converted to Christianity. In A.D. 312 the Emperor Constantine issued the Edict of Milan, which granted toleration to Christians. Later, he was himself baptized as a Christian.

At this time, the Roman Empire was in decline. Uncivilized tribes from the north called Barbarians began to threaten the borders. Meanwhile, high taxes, plagues, and civil wars disrupted life within the empire. As a result, Emperor Diocletian decided that the empire was too big for one man to rule. He divided it into two parts, an Eastern and a Western Roman Empire. The Eastern Empire included most of the Middle East and North Africa. When Constantine became emperor, he founded a new capital for the Eastern Empire at Byzantium in present-day Turkey. He named his new capital Constantinople. However, the new civilization that grew up there is known by the name of the earlier Greek town, Byzantium. Here the traditions and authority of the Roman Empire were preserved for a thousand years. Because of its location in the East, however, Byzantium also became heir to Hellenistic and Middle Eastern culture. Therefore, Byzantine civilization is different from Roman. Long after Rome fell in the West, the Middle East continued to enjoy the benefits of a rich and creative Christian civilization that combined the best of East and West.

Discussion

1. Why was Jesus seen as a threat to peace?
2. Why was Paul well suited to spread the message of Jesus?
3. Why was the Roman Empire divided into two parts?
4. How was Byzantium the heir to Roman and Hellenistic culture?

Map Activities

Using map C, locate and label the modern states of Italy, Israel, Jordan, Syria, Turkey, and Iraq. Locate and label the cities of Rome, Jerusalem, and Istanbul. Also locate and label the Dead Sea and the Mediterranean Sea. Finally, using a pen or pencil of a different color, locate and label ancient Palestine, which included the area of modern Israel and the area owned by Jordan located on the west bank of the Jordan River. Also, locate and label Constantinople, which was located where modern Istanbul is today.

Name _____ Date _____

CHALLENGES

1. To whom did the Dead Sea Scrolls belong?

_____

2. What are the main sources of information about the life of Jesus?

_____

_____

3. Why was Jesus perceived as a threat to the peace?

_____

_____

4. Who is responsible for carrying Jesus's message beyond Palestine?

_____

5. What crime did Nero blame on the Christians so that he could persecute them?

_____

6. Who was the first Roman emperor to convert to Christianity?

_____

7. Who divided the Roman Empire in half?

_____

8. What was the name of the new capital of the Eastern Roman Empire?

_____

9. What areas were included in the Eastern Roman Empire?

_____

_____

10. What was the Christian civilization in the Middle East called after the fall of Rome in the West?

_____

FROM THE SANDS OF ARABIA COMES ISLAM

The caravan slowly crept through the howling sand storm. The swirling sand stung the faces of the camel drivers as they coaxed their exhausted animals the last few miles toward the desert city of Mecca. In the lead was the young man called Mohammed. Within the first few days of the journey, he had already earned the respect of the other camel drivers for his intelligence and honesty. When they reached the Syrian city of Bostra, Mohammed proved himself an able negotiator with the traders in the market place. Now they were returning to Mecca after a successful journey.

Mohammed was no ordinary caravan driver, however. As he grew older, he would go alone out into the desert around his city of Mecca to meditate and reflect. One night in A.D. 610, as Mohammed sat in a dark cave, he heard a commanding voice say: "Read, in the

The courtyard of the Islamic Mosque of al-Azhar

name of God . . .". Terrified, Mohammed, who could neither read nor write, replied: "How can I?" The voice repeated: "Read, for the Lord is most bounteous . . . and teaches man what he did not know. . . .". Mohammed fled to his home, but still the voice followed him. He soon realized that whether he wanted to be or not, he had been chosen as a prophet of God. The revelations kept coming for the next 20 years. Later written down, they make up the 114 chapters of the book called the *Koran.* Moslems, the name given to those who follow the way of life laid out in the *Koran,* believe it to be the word of God given to Mohammed. *Islam,* which means "to submit to God," is the name given to the religion founded by Mohammed.

Islam shares many of the beliefs of Judaism and Christianity. In fact, many of the early prophets like Abraham and Moses are also held in high esteem by Moslems and are found in the *Koran.* The Moslems also believe in only one God whom they call Allah. He is the all-powerful creator of the universe and judges people according to their actions. The *Koran* also mentions Jesus, but sees him as a prophet like Mohammed.

The *Koran* requires Moslems to follow the five pillars of Islam. The first pillar is the *Shahadah.* This means that the Moslem must say and believe that there is no god but God and Mohammed is his messenger. The second pillar is *Salat.* This means worship. Five times a day, a good Moslem should face Mecca, bathe his face, arms, feet, and hands, and recite prayers. In Moslem cities men called *muzeins* announce the prayer times by singing prayers from the top of high towers called minarets. On Friday at noon, all Moslems should gather at the *mosque* and pray together. Mosques are special buildings for prayer with minarets and baths for Moslems to bathe themselves before prayer. Inside, the floors are covered with beautiful, intricate carpets. Here Moslems can kneel and touch their foreheads to the floor, which they must do when they pray. The third pillar is *Sawm,* or fasting. Each year during the month of *Ramadan,* Moslems must neither eat nor drink from sunrise to sunset. When the sun sets, Moslem families gather to celebrate Ramadan with feasts of specially prepared and delicious food. The Moslems use a lunar calendar, which means that their months advance 11 or 12 days each year in relation to our calendar.

The fourth pillar of Islam is *Zakat,* or alms. All Moslems must pay part of their income to help provide for the poor. In many Middle Eastern cities, schools, fountains, and hospitals are founded and maintained by this money. The fifth pillar of Islam is *Hajj,* or pilgrimage to Mecca. At least once in a Moslem's life, he should make the journey to Mecca. Here he performs certain rituals established by Mohammed. These include circling the *Ka'ba,* a very ancient stone enclosure, which the Moslems believe was rebuilt by Abraham; stoning a pillar that represents the Devil; and gathering on the plains of Arafat where Mohammed gave his last sermon. Today, millions of Moslems from all over the world come to Mecca on Hajj.

At first, most of the people of Mecca laughed at Mohammed and believed he was insane. Nevertheless, in time he gathered about him a group of followers who believed him to be the messenger of God. As the number of Mohammed's followers increased, he became a threat to the rulers of Mecca. His enemies even attempted to assassinate him. He was forced to seek shelter in the nearby city of Medina. Here, he won over the inhabitants by settling a dangerous dispute that divided the city. The Meccans sent armies to defeat Mohammed's followers but they were defeated in battle after battle. Eventually, Mohammed was able to return to Mecca in triumph. While still alive, Mohammed's message spread all over Arabia, but upon his death in 632, the new religion was carried throughout the Middle East.

Discussion

1. How did Mohammed appear to be unwilling, at first, to be a prophet?
2. What beliefs does Islam share with Judaism and Christianity?
3. What do Moslems do to encourage prayer?
4. Was Mohammed's message well received in Arabia?

Map Activities

Using map A, locate and label the modern states of Iran, United Arab Emirates, Saudi Arabia, Kuwait, Yemen, and Oman. Also locate and label the Persian Gulf, the Red Sea, and the Arabian Sea. Also locate and label Jiddah, Riyadh, and Sanaa. Finally, using a pen or pencil of a different color, locate and label Medina, Mecca, and the plains of Arafat just north of Mecca.

Name _____ Date _____

CHALLENGES

1. In what year did Mohammed hear the first voice?

_____

2. In what book are collected the revelations heard by Mohammed?

_____

3. What is a Moslem?

_____

4. What does Islam mean?

_____

5. What is the first pillar of Islam? Explain.

_____

_____

6. What is the second pillar of Islam? Explain.

_____

_____

7. What is the third pillar of Islam? Explain.

_____

_____

8. What is the fourth pillar of Islam? Explain.

_____

_____

9. What is the fifth pillar of Islam? Explain.

_____

_____

10. What happened to Islam after the death of Mohammed?

_____

_____

THE ISLAMIC GOLDEN AGE

Shipwrecked on an uncharted island, Sinbad searched for other humans. He decided to climb a tall tree in the hope of seeing something. Scanning the horizon at last he spotted a huge, white dome. "This must be a sign of civilization," he thought to himself. He climbed down from the tree and headed for the dome. At last, he came upon it and began to search for an entrance. He walked around it several times but could find no way in. As he stopped to scratch his head, the sun suddenly disappeared, and he found himself in shadow. At first, he thought the sun was only behind a cloud, but his heart began to pound when he discovered an enormous bird flying toward him. The giant dome was none other than an egg. Sinbad scrambled for cover.

An example of Islamic ornament from the Alhambra in Granada, Spain

The story above is taken from the second voyage of Sinbad the Sailor. It is only one of hundreds of stories to be found in *The Tales of the Arabian Nights.* The author of the *Tales* collected stories from all over the Middle East at a time when Islamic civilization was at its height. Upon the death of Mohammed, Islam spread throughout the Middle East at great speed. Within 200 years after the prophet's death, an Islamic empire spread from Iran in the east to Spain in the west. For a time, all of this was united under the control of the *caliph* in Baghdad. Caliph means "successor" to Mohammed, and it was under these men that the new religion spread.

Islam expanded quickly for many reasons. First, the Arabs were great warriors and were led by brilliant generals like Khalid ibn-al-Walid. They believed they were fighting a *jihad,* or holy war. Many Moslems believe that if they are killed in a jihad, they are certain to go to heaven. Secondly, many people in the Middle East were weary of Byzantine control. The Byzantine Empire imposed heavy taxes and was intolerant of the many splinter groups that had grown up within Christianity. The orthodox Byzantine emperors called these groups *heresies* and tried to crush them by force. Heresy was the name given by the church authorities to any belief that they thought would split the church. When the Moslems invaded these lands, they found that the inhabitants of land where heresies were prevalent would rather be controlled by Moslems than the Byzantine emperor. This view was strengthened by the fact that Islam preaches toleration of other religions. Finally, the Byzantine Empire was exhausted by warfare against the other great power of the Middle East, Persia. As a result, all of Persia and all of the Byzantine Empire except Turkey quickly fell to the caliph's warriors.

After the Islamic conquest, the Middle East enjoyed a new golden age under Islam. Because all trade routes between Europe, Asia, and Africa passed through the Middle East,

Moslem cities like Baghdad, Cairo, and Basra became thriving trade centers. Particularly, the wealth and magnificence of Baghdad became legendary. Also, non-Arabic peoples like the Persians and Egyptians were gradually merged into the empire. As a result, Moslem scholars synthesized the learning from throughout the Middle East. From the eighth to the 12th centuries, the Moslem world was a place of scholarship, scientific learning, and artistic creativity. It was during this time that *The Tales of the Arabian Nights* were composed. Moslem scholars translated and studied Greek and Persian books on philosophy, astronomy, chemistry, physics, geography, and medicine. Yet they did more than just study the work of the past. Al-Razi, a Persian scientist, was the first physician to use plaster casts to set bones. He also accurately described the symptoms of diseases like smallpox and measles. Others like Khwarizmi, an Arab mathematician, developed algebra and wrote the first book on the subject. Later it was translated into Latin and was used as a textbook in medieval European universities. Together with Khwarizmi's other works, it was responsible for introducing Arabic numerals into Europe. Still other Moslem scholars like the Spanish-born al-Idrisi revolutionized geography by creating maps representing the spherical shape of the earth.

Islamic art and architecture included objects of breathtaking beauty. As in the sciences, the Moslems borrowed from Byzantium, Persia, and even China. Yet, they went beyond these influences to synthesize and develop their own styles. Islam forbade pictures or statues of natural objects like animals and people. To compensate, Moslem artists created exquisite geometric designs to decorate their mosques. They also took the art of the beautiful handwriting, called calligraphy, and developed it into graceful and elegant decoration. In the Alhambra, one of the most beautiful palaces in the world located in Granada, Spain, modern tourists can see Islamic art and architecture at its height. Here, the last Islamic rulers of Spain surrounded themselves with decorated doors and multicolored archways borrowed from Byzantium and intricate calligraphy and brilliant geometric patterns borrowed from Persia, all combined with Spanish grace and elegance.

Discussion

1. Why did Islam spread throughout the Middle East so quickly?
2. How was the Islamic civilization similar to the Hellenistic civilization?
3. What were the main accomplishments of Islamic civilization?

Map Activities

Using map A, locate and label the modern states of Turkey, Cyprus, Syria, Jordan, Iraq, Armenia, and Azerbaijan. Locate and label the Tigris and Euphrates Rivers, the Persian Gulf, the Mediterranean Sea, the Red Sea, Damascus, Beirut, and Amman. Finally, using a pen or pencil of a different color, locate and label Cairo, Baghdad, Basra, and Constantinople. Knowing that these were important cities on the trade route between India and Europe, draw in where you think the trade routes were.

Name _____ Date _____

CHALLENGES

1. From where did the stories in *The Tales of the Arabian Nights* come?

_____

_____

2. Who controlled the Islamic Empire?

_____

3. Who was Khalid ibn-al-Walid?

_____

4. What is a heresy?

_____

5. Before the rise of Islam, what were the two great powers in the Middle East?

_____

6. Why did Middle Eastern cities become trade centers?

_____

_____

7. Who was al-Razi, and what is he known for?

_____

_____

8. Who was al-Idrisi, and what is he known for?

_____

_____

9. Why did the Moslems use geometric designs to decorate their mosques?

_____

_____

10. Where is the Alhambra?

_____

CRUSADERS DESCEND UPON THE MIDDLE EAST

The blistering heat of the summer sun made the armor of the Crusaders too hot to touch and miserable to wear. Yet, here they stood, outside Jerusalem, the Holy City itself, and the Moslem defenders appeared to be weakening. The order was given again to advance. Down the dusty slopes of their earthworks the Crusaders pushed the battering ram. Others carried ladders to mount the walls. They were met by arrows and rocks from the defenders on the walls. This time, however, the gate gave way and the attackers, sensing victory, found new strength to push into the city itself. The long years of fighting, illness, and fatigue seemed to be coming to an end. To taste success at last after so much frustration put the Crusaders into a frenzy. The

The Crusaders were successful in taking Jerusalem from the Moslems on the first crusade.

Crusaders celebrated the capture of the Holy City by massacring most of its inhabitants—Moslem, Christian, and Jew.

The capture of Jerusalem, as described above, was only one episode in a series of European invasions of the Middle East that historians call the Crusades. For many centuries before the Crusades, the Christian Church in Europe had battled for survival against pagans and even Christian kings. By the 11th century the church had emerged stronger than ever. At this point the Byzantine Emperor, Alexius Comnenus I, sent envoys to the Pope, Urban II, requesting help. Byzantium was being threatened by a new and aggressive tribe from Central Asia called the Seljuk Turks. After converting to Islam, they conquered much of the Middle East and hoped to absorb the remnants of the Byzantine Empire. Alexius Comnenus I requested military support to help defend his realm and protect Christians who wanted to go on pilgrimage to Jerusalem and lands nearby where Jesus had lived. Pilgrimage, or visiting holy places, was an important feature of medieval Christianity. The Seljuk Turks were less tolerant than the Moslem Empire before them and often attacked pilgrims. Urban II decided it was time to counterattack against the Seljuk Turks.

Urban called on all of Christian Europe to embark on a holy Crusade, or holy war, against the infidels, as the Christians called all Moslems. The support for the Crusade was tremendous. Soon, men from all over France, Italy, and Sicily were sewing crosses on their clothing and marching off to war. Historians estimate that in the first Crusade somewhere between 5,000 and 10,000 mounted knights, between 25,000 and 50,000 foot soldiers, and as many more wives, servants, families, and religious men set out for the Holy Land. Why did they go? There were many reasons. Many were filled with genuine religious zeal to recapture Jerusalem. Others, however, sought adventure and wealth. Many poor or landless knights hoped to make themselves lords or even princes.

The Crusaders encountered many unforeseen difficulties on their long journey to Palestine. Beginning in northern France, some marched overland through Germany, Hungary, and Bulgaria to Constantinople. Others took ships from Marseilles or Genoa. One of the first groups, lead by Peter the Hermit, was so badly organized that by the time they reached Bulgaria, they had to prey on fellow Christians for food. As a result, they were attacked and many were killed. When the remnants were ferried across the Bosporus by the Byzantine Emperor, they were easily massacred or captured and sold into slavery by the Turks. A second group made up of knights and soldiers lead by Godfrey of Bouillon had more success. Because it was an organized army, it arrived in Byzantium intact and went on to attack Seljuk Turkish strongholds. They captured Nicaea and Antioch after long, bloody fights, and finally, on July 5, 1099, Godfrey of Bouillon and his soldiers captured Jerusalem.

After accomplishing their objective, some Crusaders went home, but others stayed to establish Crusader states and live off their conquered wealth. Godfrey of Bouillon was named king of the Latin Kingdom of Jerusalem. Others became lords or counts. However, Christian control of Palestine was brief. Within fifty years, the Crusader states were fighting amongst themselves. After recovering from the shock of the first Crusade, Moslem warriors took advantage of these divisions to begin to win back lost territory. Finally, Saladin, one of the greatest and wisest of the Moslem princes, attacked and recaptured Jerusalem.

Many more Crusades were called over the course of the next century but all failed to win more than token victories. In fact, they tended to weaken Christian control of Byzantium. The fourth Crusade allowed itself to be distracted by the promise of Constantinople's wealth and captured the city from the Christian Byzantines in 1204. Although the Byzantines later regained control, the empire was permanently weakened and finally fell to the Turks in 1453.

The Crusades failed to conquer the Holy Land for Christian Europe, but they had far-reaching consequences. First, by exposing Europeans to the more advanced civilization of the Middle East, they forced Europe to open itself up more completely to advances in philosophy, technology, medicine, and mathematics. The Europeans had been learning from Byzantium and the Islamic world for some time, but the Crusades accelerated the process. Second, the Crusades resulted in increased trade between Europe and the Middle East. The Crusaders developed a taste for perfumes, silks, spices, jewelry, and fruits that they had never seen before. Third, the Crusades increased the pace of economic change that was already being felt in Europe. For example, banks had to be invented to supply Crusaders with credit so that they didn't have to carry money, which could be easily stolen along the way. Finally, the Crusades encouraged Europeans to develop new kinds of ships and navigation to carry Crusaders to the Holy Land. Eventually, this knowledge would enable Europeans to explore the coasts of Africa, Asia, and the Americas.

Discussion

1. What were the causes of the Crusades?
2. Why did so many Europeans want to go on a Crusade?
3. How do you think the Crusades affected the people of the Middle East?
4. What were the long-term results of the Crusades for the Europeans?

Name _____ Date _____

CHALLENGES

1. How did those on the first Crusade celebrate the capture of Jerusalem?

_____

2. Who was the Byzantine emperor who asked for aid from the Pope?

_____

3. Who were the Seljuk Turks?

_____

4. What was a pilgrimage?

_____

5. Who called on all Christians to embark on a Crusade?

_____

6. What happened to the group of Crusaders led by Peter the Hermit?

_____

7. Why was Godfrey of Bouillon successful?

_____

8. Who recaptured Jerusalem from the Crusaders?

_____

9. On which Crusade did the Europeans capture Constantinople?

_____

10. What resulted from the Europeans' increased knowledge of ships and navigation?

_____

_____

Map Activities

    Using map C, locate and label the modern states of France, Italy, Germany, Hungary, Bulgaria, and Syria. Locate and label the Bosphorus, the Black Sea, and the Mediterranean Sea. Using a pen or pencil of a different color, locate and label Constantinople; Bouillon, which is on the southern border of Belgium; Palestine, which included the area of modern-day Israel and the west bank of the Jordan River now owned by Jordan; Antioch, which is modern Antakya in Turkey; and Nicaea, near the modern city of Goynuk, Turkey. Trace the routes followed by Peter the Hermit and Godfrey de Bouillon.

THE MIDDLE EAST UNDER THE POWER OF THE TURKS

Suleiman the Magnificent

The Serbian boys cried as they saw their village for the last time. They were being carried off as part of the *devshirme,* or boy tax. Each year the Turkish governor of Serbia demanded that his Christian subjects supply the sultan with boys between the ages of 8 and 10 as slaves. Now the boys pondered the fact that their turn had come as they saw the village disappear behind the mountain. Their parents, watching from the village, could console themselves with a few good thoughts. Although the boys would be converted to Islam, they would probably get the best education possible and be almost assured of wealth and status as servants of the Ottoman sultan.

Who were these Ottomans, and where did they come from? After the Middle Easterners had successfully fought off the Crusaders, they faced a more fearsome enemy: the Mongols. These ferocious warriors mounted on short, sturdy horses trotted into the Middle East after conquering China. They swept all before them and burned and looted great Islamic cities like Baghdad. Yet, their domination was short-lived. Osman, a prince of a small Turkish principality in the 15th century, gradually carved out for himself a new empire from the remnant of the old. Named after Osman, this new empire is known as the Ottoman Empire. With amazing speed, his successors, with names like Mehmet the Conqueror or Selim the Inexorable, spread the empire in all directions. After Turkey, they turned to the Serbian Empire, then captured Constantinople, bringing the Byzantine Empire to an end. Finally, they captured all of the Middle East and North Africa. In 1529 the greatest of Osman's descendants, Suleiman the Magnificent, even attacked Vienna, one of the main capitals of Europe.

Although Suleiman failed to capture the Austrian city, he nevertheless ruled over a well-run empire from his capital in Istanbul. When the Ottomans captured Constantinople, they changed the name to Istanbul and proceeded to make an already beautiful city breathtaking. They built mosques with huge domes and pencil-thin minarets. For the first 200 years of its existence, the Ottoman Empire was ruled by able sultans. These men could count also on the fanatical loyalty of the slaves collected by the devshirme. They supplied the empire with administrators, scribes, and soldiers. Most noteworthy of these slaves were the Janissaries. Like the rest of the devshirme, they came as children from the sultan's Christian possessions. Well-educated in special schools, they made up an elite corps of infantry. The Janissaries were kept in closed barracks where they spent their time in endless military drill. They were only allowed out to fight the sultan's enemies. Because of their discipline and devotion to the sultan, they were almost unbeatable in battle.

However, even in Suleiman's day, the empire began to show signs of weakness. The Ottomans fell behind the Europeans in technology. While the Europeans developed new and faster sailing ships, the Ottomans still used oar-driven galleys. Conservative religious leaders repressed the use of printing presses so that books were rare. In time, even the Janissaries were no match for European armies with better firearms. Meanwhile, European discoverers found new sea-born trade routes around the coast of Africa and across the Atlantic to the New World. Sea travel was much cheaper than carrying goods by land across the Middle East. As a result, commerce and trade in the Ottoman Empire deteriorated. Most of the trade that survived was dominated by European merchants who negotiated special contracts called *capitulations*. These insured that they paid no tax and enjoyed special privileges that put their Middle Eastern competitors out of business.

Corruption, too, had weakened the sultan's ability to rule. With the death of Suleiman, the line of strong sultans came to an end. Suleiman's heir was known as Selim the Drunkard. The office of the grand vizier, the sultan's right-hand man, came to be occupied by men chosen for their popularity, not their ability. Without strong control at the top, administrators taxed the people unjustly for profit, and the Janissaries began to dominate the sultan. When the sultans tried to initiate reforms, they were assassinated by the Janissaries who feared losing their privileges. In the various provinces of the empire such as Egypt, local governors gained increasing power from the sultan so that they became almost separate princes. As the world entered the 19th century, the Middle East found itself running desperately behind Europe.

Discussion

1. What advantages did the Ottoman sultans gain from the devshirme?
2. Why was the Ottoman Empire so powerful at first?
3. What caused the Ottoman Empire to decline?

Map Activities

Using map C, locate and label the modern states of Serbia, Bosnia, Croatia, Austria, Turkey, and Russia. Also locate the Black Sea, the Caspian Sea, the Jordan River, the Nile River, and the Dardanelles, the island of Crete, the Aegean Sea, and the Caucasus Mountains. Also locate the cities of Ankara and Beirut. Using a pen or pencil of a different color, locate and label Vienna, Istanbul, and Baghdad. Using the text, draw in the boundaries of the Ottoman Empire as best you can.

Name _____ Date _____

CHALLENGES

1. What was the devshirme?

_____

2. After the Crusades were over, who invaded the Middle East?

_____

3. Who founded the Ottoman Empire?

_____

4. Who was the greatest of the Ottoman sultans?

_____

5. Who were the Janissaries?

_____

_____

6. What was the new name of Constantinople?

_____

7. What ruined Middle Eastern trade?

_____

_____

8. Who was Suleiman's heir?

_____

9. How did the Janissaries block reforms?

_____

10. By the 19th century, what was the relationship of the Middle East to Europe?

_____

_____

NEW FORCES FOR CHANGE IN THE OTTOMAN EMPIRE

The Turkish ambassador tried to repress his feelings of humiliation as the ambassador from Russia pushed the final draft of the treaty to his side of the table. In it he read how the Ottoman Empire promised to turn almost all of the shore of the Black Sea, including the Crimean Peninsula, over to Russia. He hated to sign the document, which recorded only the latest of the sultan's losses to Russia, but he had no choice. Even as the diplomats haggled over the terms of the treaty, a Russian army was marching towards Istanbul.

In the final years of the 18th and the beginning of the 19th century, the Ottoman Empire became a battleground. As we can see, Russia sought to acquire Ottoman

Muhammad Ali declared Egypt independent from the Ottoman Empire.

territory along its frontier. France, too, sent Napoleon Bonaparte to invade Egypt. The invasion failed, but it had profound effects. Napoleon brought with him scholars who began to study, for the first time, the ancient remains of Egypt. They also found the Rosetta Stone, which enabled them to decipher Egyptian hieroglyphics. They could do this because the same text was written both in Greek and Egyptian hieroglyphics on the stone.

For the people of the Middle East, Napoleon's invasion impressed upon them the superior technological capabilities of a European power. Before Napoleon, they still believed that they were the most sophisticated civilization in the world. The ease with which Napoleon's troops defeated the Egyptian army in the heart of the Middle East was a great shock. After Napoleon was driven out with British help, Middle Easterners redoubled their pleas for reform and modernization.

Despairing that the Ottomans would never improve the system, Muhammad Ali, the governor of Egypt, declared Egypt independent. He began a crash program of modernization along European lines. He set up schools of military science, medicine, and engineering. He founded government printing presses to publish technical manuals. He also began to publish the first Arab-language newspaper in 1828 called *al-Waqai al-Misriyyah,* which translates as "The Official Gazette." Soon other Arabic-language newspapers were springing up in Syria, Palestine, and Lebanon, helping to foster a new awareness of what it was to be an Arab. Such developments helped to foster a growing sense of *nationalism* among the people of the Middle East.

Around the same time, Greece rebelled and eventually broke free from the Ottoman yoke. This was only the beginning. Nationalism, which is the belief that a particular group of people sharing the same language and culture should form an independent state,

76

became popular in the Balkans. European powers like Russia and Britain, eager to gain an advantage at the expense of the Ottoman Empire, supported various nationalist groups. In time, the Ottomans lost most of their European possessions. The European powers sometimes even fought over control of Ottoman territory. During the Crimean War from 1854 to 1856, Russia fought Britain, France, and Sardinia for possession of Ottoman territories in the Balkans. The governor of Egypt tried to compete with the Europeans by building the Suez Canal. This created a waterway for ships between the Mediterranean and the Red Sea. The Canal was finally completed in 1869 but at great cost. The Egyptians had to borrow huge amounts of money from the French and British to complete it. In 1882 Britain used Egypt's inability to pay off its debts as an excuse to invade and occupy Egypt for the next 60 years.

The humiliations suffered by the Ottomans finally persuaded men in power to seek dramatic reforms like those first tried in Egypt. Ali Pasha, who became the grand vizier, or prime minister, of the Sultan Abdul Aziz, launched a program of reforms called the Tanzimat. But the demand for change only increased. Meanwhile, nationalism spread to all parts of the Middle East. Finally, in 1908 a group of reformers called the Young Turks rebelled against the deeply conservative sultan, Abdulhamid II. The beginning of the 20th century saw the old sultan replaced by his more cooperative brother, Mehmet V, and a new government formed under the control of the Young Turks. Although facing enormous problems, they were determined to bring what was left of the Ottoman Empire into the 20th century.

Discussion

1. What resulted from Napoleon's invasion of Egypt?
2. How did Muhammad Ali try to reform Egypt?
3. What helped foster nationalism in the Middle East?
4. How did European powers take advantage of nationalism within the Ottoman Empire? Why?

Map Activities

Using map C, locate and label the modern states of Egypt, Syria, Lebanon, Greece, Bulgaria, Serbia, Montenegro, Bosnia, England, France, Russia, and Turkey. Also locate the Black Sea and the Bosporus, the Mediterranean Sea, and the cities of Alexandria, Tbilisi, Ankara, and Odessa. Using a pen or pencil of a different color, locate and label the island of Sardinia (which later came to dominate the kingdom of Italy), the area known as the Balkans, and the Crimean Peninsula. Draw in and label the Suez Canal.

Name _____ Date _____

CHALLENGES

1. What territories did the Russians take from the Turks?

_____

2. What impact did the invasion of Egypt have on the people of the Middle East?

_____

_____

3. What was the Rosetta Stone?

_____

_____

4. What was the *al-Waqai al-Misriyyah*?

_____

5. Where did nationalism become popular?

_____

6. What countries were involved in the Crimean War?

_____

7. What was the Tanzimat?

_____

8. Who were the Young Turks?

_____

9. What did the Young Turks try to accomplish?

_____

_____

10. Whom did the Young Turks replace with Mehmet V?

_____

WORLD WAR I AND THE MIDDLE EAST

A bullet was fired at Sarajevo, Bosnia, on June 28, 1914, and Austrian Archduke Franz Ferdinand slumped over dead. No one could have imagined that this event would lead to a war of such proportions that it would be named World War I. For the Middle East, it was the beginning of a new era.

As was true in parts of Africa, the European powers had struggled for influence in the Middle East for many years. A German company received permission to build a railroad in Turkey from the Bosporus to Ankara; the next year, it got control of the Oriental railroad connecting Austria with Constantinople. Germany wanted to extend the railroad to Baghdad, but Prime

The Ottoman Army in World War I

Minister Bismarck feared that would cause problems with Russia. The German king, the Kaiser, ignored Bismarck's concerns, and in 1898, he persuaded Turkey to allow a railroad to be built to Baghdad. Russia and England both opposed it, Russia because they feared Germany might block their entrance to the Black Sea, and England because it threatened their interests in Persia and India. The British offered protection to the sheik of Kuwait, who promised to make no deals without British approval.

Turkey was often referred to as the "Sick Man of Europe," a reputation it had earned because it was ruled by an incompetent council, held power over its Christian and Arab subjects by brutal force, and stank with corruption. The Young Turks, long critical of their predecessors, were no more able to reform the Ottoman Empire than those they had replaced. The real leaders, Talaat Pasha and War Minister Enver Pasha, were not smart enough to realize the risks they were taking in foreign policy. They were eager to get into Europe's war on Germany's side, thinking that with the Kaiser's help they could seize land in the Caucasus region from Russia. In August 1914 they signed a secret alliance with Germany and waited until October to announce it. By getting involved, they were going to cross England, Russia, and France.

When World War I began, Turkey was brutally expelling Greeks from their soil, and tension was growing with Greece. The United States sold Greece two old battleships that were better than any ships in the Turkish navy. The Turks had paid the British to build two battleships for them, but they had not been delivered before the war began. Lord of the Admiralty Winston Churchill decided not to send the ships because England needed them; he did not know that Turkey had already signed on the enemy side. Two German cruisers sailed to Turkey, where they flew the Turkish flag, but the captains and crews were Germans. These ships were able to keep the Russians from breaking through the Bosporus to the Mediterranean. Russia asked England for help, and England was eager to get involved.

The British navy was converting to ships powered by oil and needed to keep Middle Eastern oil fields in friendly hands. Churchill pushed hard for an invasion of the Gallipoli Peninsula; if successful, they could attack Constantinople. An English army was raised for the attack, and the soldiers were thrilled by the opportunity; "Gallipoli fever" spread through the confident men. The Turks, trained by the Germans, were also eager for a fight. Their leader, General Mustapha Kemal, told them: "I don't order you to attack; I order you to die." The invaders suffered 20,000 casualties, and the attack stalled. Public reaction in Great Britian grew so angry that the prime minister fired Churchill. A new attack was planned and carried out, but eventually the British, Australian, and New Zealand troops were withdrawn.

Thomas E. Lawrence was more successful. A scholar, he had traveled through Syria on foot while studying Crusader architecture. He knew the language, culture, and people. When World War I broke out, he was sent to Egypt, where he began organizing the Arab Bureau. His purpose was to organize Arabs unhappy under Turkish rule. He made friends with Emir (Prince) Feisal, and persuaded him to help drive the Turks from Arab soil. With the support of General Edmund Allenby, his guerilla warfare nearly cut the railroad to Damascus. In a war short on heroes, he was known as "Lawrence of Arabia." The Arabs had supported the British and expected the British to be on their side after the war. Lawrence would later criticize Britain for not protecting the Arab interests better.

After war began between Britain and Turkey in November 1914, a British-Indian army was sent to Iraq, and it captured the Turkish fort at Fao (southern tip of Iraq). The purpose of the expedition was to keep the oil fields from enemy use, keep the Germans from using Basra as a submarine base, and protect India from German attack. In 1917 the British captured Baghdad. When Russia withdrew from the war and pulled their troops out of northeastern Iraq, the British moved northward, taking Kirkuk in May 1918. As the war was coming to an end, the British were near Mosul (northwestern Iraq). After Turkey surrendered, the British took Mosul. Persia (Iran) was barely independent, with Russia willing and able to force its will on its southern neighbor. England and France had agreed in 1907 to divide influence there, with Russia strong in northern Persia. When the Persians tried to take control of their own affairs, the Russian army marched into Tehran. With Germany as a threat, the British ignored terrible crimes committed by Russian troops against Iranians.

When the war ended with German surrender, the fates of Germany, Austria-Hungary, and Turkey were going to be decided by the victors. Whatever they decided was going to have a major effect on the Middle East.

Discussion

1. Why was the Turkish policy of supporting Germany risky?
2. How did the German ships flying the Turkish flag create serious problems for Turkey?
3. Why was guerilla warfare in the desert especially effective?
4. What happened that made the English position in the Middle East stronger by the end of the war?

Name _____   Date _____

CHALLENGES

1. Why did Bismarck oppose the idea of building a railroad to Baghdad?

_____

2. Why did Russia oppose building the railroad to Baghdad?

_____

3. Why did Talaat Pasha want to join the war on Germany's side?

_____

4. Why did Churchill refuse to deliver Turkey's battleships?

_____

5. What was "Gallipoli fever"?

_____

6. Why was the British navy concerned about the Middle East?

_____

7. Who created the Arab Bureau?

_____

8. Why was Lawrence angry with the British government after the war?

_____

_____

9. Who had control of most of Iraq at the end of World War I?

_____

10. What nation threatened Iranian independence at the end of the war?

_____

Map Activities

    Using map A, locate and label Serbia, Albania, Armenia, Qatar, Kuwait, Iran, Greece, Syria, and Iraq. Also, locate the Caucasus Mountains, the Bosporus, and the Black Sea. Also, locate Tehran, Baghdad, Kirkuk, Mosul, Damascus, Ankara, and Sarajevo. Using a pen or pencil of a different color, locate Fao, which was the far southern tip of Iraq, and the Gallipoli Peninsula, which is near the modern Turkish city of Gelibolu.

THE MANDATE SYSTEM

Three men sat around a table at Versailles discussing the future of the world. We have all thought about how we would improve the world if we could, but their conversations were different. Those three men had the power to decide how millions of people in Europe, Asia, Africa, and the Middle East were going to be ruled in the years ahead.

The idealist, President Woodrow Wilson, thought war was a terrible thing, and he was determined that World War I was going to be the last of its kind. When the United States entered World War I in 1917, he said: "The world must be made safe for democracy." To make that happen, he proposed his famous Fourteen Points to bring about world peace.

Mustapha Kemal, President of Turkey

Three of the Points were especially important to the Middle East. Point 5 said that colonial claims must be considered with equal weight given to the interests of the people affected and to the government that would rule them. Point 12 said that Turkey should be independent, and other peoples ruled by Turkey should have self-rule. Point 14 called for "a general association of nations" (this became the League of Nations) to guarantee independence to great and small nations alike.

Prime Minister David Lloyd George of Great Britain wanted to take control of German colonies around the world. Premier Georges Clemenceau of France was less interested in colonies than in punishing Germany by taking some of its land and making it pay the cost of the war. The conference decided German colonies could not be made free, but were to become "mandates" of "advanced nations." Each year, the "tutor" would report to the League of Nations about how the "student" was progressing.

All of the mandates in the Middle East were given to England and France, and the desires of the people for independence were ignored. This is a brief summary of what happened in the Middle East from 1920 to 1939.

TURKEY went through major changes. Mustapha Kemal (Ataturk) replaced the sultan in 1922 and ruled as president of Turkey and president-general of the National People's Party. The legislature was no problem for him—he chose all its members himself. Under his rule, polygamy ended. Women no longer had to wear veils and were allowed to go to school. Highways and railroads were built, and industry expanded.

SYRIA and LEBANON were French mandates. The French had trouble controlling Syria because French officials were high handed and the people were determined to be free. In 1925 French tanks rolled against rebels in Damascus, killing about 1,000 people. Syria was allowed to write a constitution in 1930 that permitted France to control Syria's foreign policy. Lebanon was different from other Middle Eastern countries. It had a large

Christian population, and even the Turks had allowed them freedom in economic matters. In 1941 Lebanon finally received full independence. It was not until 1945 that Syria received its freedom.

TRANSJORDAN, the region east of Palestine, was a British mandate until 1946 ruled by King Abdullah. This mandate ran smoothly.

IRAQ was also a British mandate ruled by Emir Feisal, the brother of Transjordan's king. Much progress was made in Iraq: a parliament began, transportation and communications greatly improved, and its oil resources were developed. By 1936 it was the eighth-leading oil producer in the world. There were serious problems, however. The people strongly resented British rule. Relations with Turkey were poor, and they argued over where to draw the boundary. In 1932 Iraq was given its independence. After King Feisal's death in 1933, the nation was troubled by riots, a massacre of hundreds of Christians by Iraqi troops, and efforts to topple the government. The Germans and Italians used the confusion in Iraq to advantage, adding to British concerns about how to handle Iraq.

IRAN was still independent, but its fabulous oil wealth was controlled by the British-owned Anglo-Iranian Oil Company. In 1925 Reza Khan came to power as Shah and modernized the nation. He replaced religious courts with regular courts. He expanded education and created the first university in the country in 1934. He increased the number of roads from 2,000 miles to 15,000 miles and built the 1,000-mile-long Trans-Iranian railroad. In 1937 the Shah gave American companies the right to develop oil fields in eastern Iran. A few Iranians got rich, but most were as poor as ever.

ARABIA. The most important leader of that desert region was Ibn Saud, an imposing and able leader who took the warring tribes of the desert and built them into a nation. Between the wars, the only important trade came from tourists going to the Moslem holy cities. Oil fields were just beginning to be developed, and in 1936 Saudi Arabia produced only 1.25 million barrels. The first automobile reached Saudi Arabia in 1926, and in 1930 there were still only 1,500 cars in the country.

EGYPT had its own king, but the British military controlled the country. In 1936 British troops left Cairo, but 10,000 troops and 400 planes remained to protect the Suez Canal.

Throughout the Middle East, Western influence was growing, with Great Britain, France, and the United States increasingly involved in the affairs of the region. More progressive people of the region saw the need to modernize, but conservatives feared that traditions were in danger of being lost forever.

Discussion

1. As a ruler wanting to modernize a nation like Turkey or Iran, what kinds of arguments would you hear opposing change?
2. In the long run, were mandates better for the Middle East than immediate freedom would have been?
3. As the ruler wanting to change Iran, where would you begin: roads, schools, democratic government, or laws making women equal? Why?
4. How was oil going to change the Middle East?

Name _____ Date _____

CHALLENGES

1. Was it clear whether Point 5 would help the people living in colonies? Why or why not?

_____

_____

2. As an Arab living in Ottoman Turkey, would you be encouraged by Point 12? Why or why not? _____

_____

3. Which leader seemed most interested in inheriting German colonies?

_____

4. How was a mandate like a colony?

_____

5. As a Turkish woman, what did Ataturk do for you?

_____

6. What area of Syrian life did the French control after 1930?

_____

7. Which country was independent first, Syria or Lebanon?

_____

8. Which nation dominated Iraq? Why was it increasingly important?

_____

_____

9. What Middle Eastern leader was Shah Reza Khan most similar to? In what way?

_____

_____

10. What was Saudi Arabia's importance before oil came along?

_____

Map Activities

    Using map A, locate and label Turkey, Syria, Iraq, Azerbaijan, Iran, Saudi Arabia, and Egypt. Also locate and label the Tigris and Euphrates Rivers, the Sinai, the Gulf of Aqaba, and the Mediterranean Sea. Also, locate the cities of Tehran, Istanbul, Damascus, Beirut, Baghdad, Jeddah, and Cairo. Finally, using a pen or pencil of a different color, put GB on those countries dominated by Great Britain and F on those countries dominated by France.

THE MIDDLE EAST AND WORLD WAR II

As the nations of Europe and Asia moved closer to war in the 1930s, the Middle East became important again. Middle Eastern oil could be a big factor in deciding which side won the war. Also vital was the need for a supply line to Russia which could best be reached by a route through Iran.

Turkey had learned its lesson in World War I and had no intention of getting involved. When Germany's westward advance was stopped at the English Channel, Hitler's need for oil caused him to develop a bold but risky policy that involved the Middle East. Germany would go around Turkey. One army was to drive into Russia, and after punching its way through the Caucasus and Georgia, it could reach the oil fields from the north.

A German panzer crew surrenders to British troops at the Battle of El Alamein in October 1942.

The other army was to attack Egypt, and after reaching the Suez Canal, nothing could stop it from reaching the oil fields from the south. At first, it looked like the plan was working. In 1942 General Erwin Rommel's Afrika Korps reached El Alamein, only 70 miles from Cairo. The German advance into Russia succeeded in reaching Stalingrad. That was as far as either army advanced, however.

Four areas of the Middle East were going to be especially important to the United States and Great Britain after the war ended.

IRAQ. When World War II began in 1939, Iraq was ruled by a three-year-old king. The most powerful leader in the country was Nuri al-Sa'id. Nuri was too pro-British to suit many officers in the army, who admired the success of the Germans. A group known as the "Four Colonels" overthrew Nuri in 1941 and made Rashid Ali the premier. Within a month, the British began working to overthrow Rashid. With a small army marching out of Transjordan, they defeated a much larger Iraqi army, and Rashid was forced into exile. Nuri returned to power, and the government declared war on Germany in 1943. The Four Colonels remained heroes in the minds of many Iraqis, however, because they tried to free the country from British influence.

SAUDI ARABIA was officially neutral in the war until 1945, but from the beginning, it favored England. During the war, the flow of tourists to Mecca and Medina dropped drastically, and the nation was in a terrible financial slump. Great Britain and the United States gave them money to keep the country running. The United States had four good reasons to help the Saudis: (1) growing concern over the amount of oil being pumped from American fields, (2) future interests of the Arabian-American Oil Company (ARAMCO),

(3) the desire to keep military bases on Arabian soil, and (4) to keep the friendship of the king.

IRAN. The best route for sending aid to Russia was through Iran, and the United States and Great Britain joined Russia in interfering in Iranian affairs. The Tudeh Party was an Iranian version of the Communist Party and was very active. To counter Russian influence in northern Iran, the British moved troops into southern Iran. The British and Russians agreed that their troops were to leave Iran six months after the war ended. The United States also sent a few troops and advisers to help Iran handle its finances and internal security.

PALESTINE. For centuries, Jews around the world dreamed of the day when Palestine would be theirs again. That idea was strengthened when Russia's czars began *pogroms,* government-approved attacks on Jewish people and property. These caused millions of Jews to go to the United States, but others planned for a return to Palestine. Leaders like Leo Pinsker and Theodor Herzl saw the need for a Jewish nation in the 19th century.

In 1917 the British cabinet approved the Balfour Declaration: "His Majesty's Government view with favour the establishment in Palestine of a National Home for the Jewish people and will use their best endeavours to facilitate the achievement of this objective, it being clearly understood that nothing shall be done which may prejudice the civil and religious rights of existing non-Jewish communities in Palestine." This was very vague, and how it could be achieved was a mystery.

Jews began moving to Palestine after World War I, buying land from absentee landlords. The number of Jews in Palestine was 174,000 in 1931, but rose to 382,000 by 1936. Palestinian Arabs, feeling threatened by their lack of influence with the British government and by the growing number of Jewish settlers, rioted in 1936, and the British agreed to limit Jewish immigration. In 1937 the Peel Commission was sent to Palestine; it recommended that Palestine be divided into one nation for Jews and another for Arabs. Jewish leaders, however, thought the amount of land allowed them by the plan was too small, and they opposed it.

Other Arabs were growing concerned about Palestine, and Great Britain knew they would need Arab oil in case of a war with Germany. So British leaders issued the "white paper of 1939," saying that it was not their policy that Palestine should become a Jewish State. During World War II, Zionist groups inside Palestine pressured Britain to leave by attacking British troops. Terror organizations like the Irgun, led by Menachem Begin, and the Lehi (Stern Group) also made occasional attacks. Public pressure in the United States and Britain wanted the mandate ended and a Jewish State created. In 1947 the United Nations approved a new State of Israel, and on May 14, 1948, it was born.

Discussion

1. Do you think any major war today would involve the Middle East? Why?
2. What risk was any government in the Middle East running by either letting the British control their affairs or in opposing the British?
3. As a Jew, how would you have interpreted the Balfour Declaration? As an Arab, what would you think it meant?

Name _____ Date _____

CHALLENGES

1. Hitler planned two attacks to reach the oil fields of the Middle East. Where were they stopped?

_____

2. Why was Nuri unpopular with officers in the Iraqi army?

_____

3. Why were the Four Colonels popular in Iraq, even though they failed?

_____

4. Why was Saudi Arabia in a financial slump because of the war?

_____

_____

5. What oil company operated in Saudi Arabia?

_____

6. What was the Iranian version of the Communist Party called?

_____

7. Why were British and Russian troops in Iran?

_____

8. Was the Balfour Declaration more popular with Jews or Arabs? Why?

_____

_____

9. Why did Britain change its policy toward Palestine in 1939?

_____

10. What were Irgun and Lehi?

_____

_____

Map Activities

    Using map A, locate and label Armenia, Georgia, Iraq, Serbia, Russia, Syria, Saudi Arabia, Iran, Israel, Jordan, and Egypt. Also, locate and label the Caucasus Mountains, the Mediterranean Sea, the Red Sea, the Persian Gulf, and the Tigris and Euphrates Rivers. Also, locate and label Cairo, Jerusalem, Basrah, Kuwait, and Esfahan. Finally, using a pen or pencil of a different color, locate and label El Alamein in Egypt, the Suez Canal, Mecca, and Medina.

ISRAEL: THE NEW KID ON THE BLOCK

A tough and determined new kid moved to the Middle Eastern block in 1948 and was going to have to fight in order to survive there. He knew what he was up against and moved quickly to prepare for the struggle.

The Jewish underground army in Palestine, the *Haganah,* had armed itself with modern weapons from Europe; its officers were well trained, and many had combat experience. There were no illusions about an easy start; the Arab nations had left no doubt that they were determined to wipe Israel off the face of the earth.

Trouble began May 15, 1948, the day after Israel officially moved in. Five

David Ben-Gurion, Israel's first prime minister

Arab nations, from Egypt to Iraq, contributed troops to attacks on Israel, but these were poorly planned, and within a year, all the nations agreed to an armistice with Israel. During that war, many Arabs left Israel, but no Arab nation wanted them, and they ended up in camps behind barbed wire. By 1949 the Arab population of Israel had dropped from the 1.3 million it had been in 1946 to only 160,000. Those who had lost their homes or who were born in the camps that were set up had bitter feelings against Israel and the United States, whom they blamed for creating Israel. Between 1948 and January 1, 1956, 771,000 Jews moved to Israel.

The government of Israel was democratic. From 1949 to 1963 the prime minister was David Ben-Gurion. The legislature, the *Knesset,* included members from many different parties, the largest being the Mapai. Since it did not have a majority, the Mapai was forced to make deals with the smaller parties to get anything done.

Surrounded by enemy nations, Israel built up its military strength. Men served three years in the army and then served in the reserves. Unmarried women served 20 months and then entered the reserves. The Israeli navy in 1968 included two destroyers and four submarines. Their air force had 350 of the most advanced planes available and some of the best pilots in the world.

EGYPT. Although the United States was friendly toward Israel, it also tried being friendly with other nations in the region. Egypt's ruler after 1954 was Gamal Abdul Nasser, who had ideas about making his nation stronger. His grand dream was to build the Aswan Dam on the Nile River to increase Egypt's electrical output and prevent the annual floods. The United States and Great Britain agreed to pay for the first studies, but Nasser hinted that he might see if the Russians would give him a better deal. The United States and Britain withdrew their offer to help. Nasser then angrily threatened to seize the Suez Canal from

88

its British and French stockholders. Israel attacked Egypt on October 29, and British and French paratroops landed near the canal on October 31, 1956. Russia, seeing the opportunity to win friends with the Arabs, threatened to send "volunteers" to help Egypt. President Eisenhower used U.S. influence against its allies in the United Nations, and a cease-fire was arranged.

SYRIA was a nation divided by religion (it had a large Christian minority), between those who looked to Egypt and those who preferred Iraqi leadership, and by those who preferred modern and those favoring traditional Arab lifestyles. The largest Syrian political party was the Bath [Ba-kth], and it favored Arab unity. In 1957 the Bath Party asked Nasser to unite the two countries, and they joined in 1958 as the United Arab Republic (UAR). The union did not work, and in 1961 the UAR broke up.

IRAQ was still a nation with only a few wealthy landowners and a vast majority of people who were very poor. In 1958 a coup (rebellion inside a government) led by Colonel Qasim took the lives of the king and his advisors. This was the beginning of a constant struggle for power, as one ruler after another was overthrown. Adding to tension was the desire of Iraqi Kurds to unite with other Kurds in Iran and Turkey to form their own nation. Meanwhile, Iraq's foreign policy turned away from Britain and the United States toward Russia.

JORDAN, east of Israel, was now home to thousands of Palestinian refugees. In 1953 King Hussein became ruler of that troubled land. There were many attempts to kill him or overthrow his government, but he held firm with the help of his army. Inside Egypt, Syria, Iraq, and Jordan was one unifying thought: to destroy the State of Israel.

THE 1967 WAR. In 1966 Syria began picking fights with Israel, and Israel responded with air raids. Egypt agreed to help Syria, and Nasser closed the Suez Canal to Israeli ships. Jordan joined the other Arabs. In a war lasting only six days, Israel captured the entire Sinai desert to the east bank of the Suez Canal, Jordan's territory west of the Jordan River (the West Bank), and the Golan Heights from Syria. Israel offered to trade the captured land for peace treaties, but the defeated neighbors refused.

The Palestine Liberation Organization (PLO) was an outgrowth of this war. In 1969 it chose Yasir Arafat as its leader. So many Palestinians in Jordan joined the PLO that they threatened King Hussein's control of his own nation. In 1970 his troops put down the PLO, which moved its operations to Lebanon instead.

THE YOM KIPPUR WAR of 1973. Egypt and Syria jointly attacked Israel at the beginning of its Yom Kippur religious observance (October 6, 1973) and caught Israel completely off guard. After some territory had been taken, the Israelis regrouped and stormed back. They not only recovered the ground they had lost, but drove the Egyptians beyond the Suez Canal, and now Israel held both of its banks.

Guns had not worked, but the Arabs now found a new weapon: oil.

Discussion

1. As a Palestinian forced to leave Israel, would you blame your troubles on Israel or on the failure of the nations that attacked in 1948? Why?
2. The U.S. Congress has two major parties, the Knesset has many, and none has a majority. Which do you think has the most problems in getting legislation passed? Why?
3. As an Israeli, how would you feel about the political problems of Syria, Iraq, and Jordan?

Name _____ Date _____

CHALLENGES

1. What was the name of the Jewish underground army?

_____

2. What happened to Israel's Arab population during the 1948 war?

_____

3. Who was the leader of Israel from 1949 to 1963?

_____

4. What is the name of Israel's legislature, and what party was strongest in its early days?

_____

5. Why did Nasser want the Aswan Dam?

_____

_____

6. What three countries attacked Egypt in October 1956?

_____

7. What country did Syria unite with for a short time? What was the new nation called?

_____

8. What group wanted to separate from Iraq? What other countries had large minorities of
that group? _____

_____

9. What regions were captured by Israel in the 1967 War?

_____

10. Why was the PLO driven from Jordan?

_____

_____

Map Activities

Using map A, locate and label Israel, Egypt, Syria, Kuwait, Georgia, Iraq, Jordan, and
Lebanon. Also, locate and label Cairo, Jerusalem, Damascus, Beirut, and Baghdad. Also,
locate and label the Nile River, the Jordan River, the Dead Sea, and the Red Sea. Using
a pen or pencil of a different color, locate and label the Aswan Dam, which is just below the
modern Egyptian city of Aswan; Lake Nasser; the Suez Canal; the Gaza Strip; and the Golan
Heights.

OIL BRINGS CHANGES TO THE MIDDLE EAST

Generations in every country share different experiences. Your grandparents lived through times that seem like ancient history to you. But think of the changes that occurred between 1940 and 1980 in the Middle East. The grandfather's camel was replaced by the grandson's car. The grandfather was uneducated, his grandson had a college degree. Grandfather had fought his wars with a sword, the grandson piloted a jet fighter. The world ignored the grandfather, but it paid close attention to the grandson. The difference between the generations was the power of oil.

In 1960 a trade organization called the Organization of Petroleum Exporting Countries (OPEC) was formed by Iran, Iraq, Ku-

Oil production has made the Middle East a major factor in world economics and politics.

wait, Saudi Arabia, and Venezuela. By 1973, OPEC had grown to 13 members interested in raising oil prices. Oil was not only improving the Middle East's standard of living, but building the fast-growing economies of Japan, Europe, and the United States. Gasoline was cheap, which inspired manufacturers to build cars getting only 12 to 15 miles per gallon. Home insulation wasn't needed when fuel oil sold at 12 cents a gallon. Wasted energy resources could not be replaced, however, and sooner or later, producer and consumer were going to pay for the extravagance.

On January 1, 1973, oil sold for $2.74 a barrel (55 gallons); a year later, it sold for $11.65. This 400-percent increase was due to Arab reaction to the 1973 war between Israel and its neighbors. When the war began, President Nixon sent $2.2 billion worth of military aid to Israel. Saudi Arabia responded by cutting all oil shipments to the United States and Europe. OPEC announced it was reducing oil production. Lines formed at gas pumps in the United States, and consumers used to paying 26 cents a gallon now paid 40 to 50 cents. This price increase sent shock waves through the economies of Asia, Europe, and the United States. The United States had its own oil resources, but many countries were completely dependent on Arab oil. When OPEC met, the powerful nations held their breath.

How did this new wealth and influence affect the region?

SAUDI ARABIA, still in many ways a traditional Arab nation, stood at the top of the class for oil reserves, with Iran third, Kuwait fourth, and other Persian Gulf nations fifth. The only outside nation in the top five was Russia, and the United States ranked seventh. To the common people of Saudi Arabia, life went on pretty much as before: prayer five times a day, women wearing long black veils, and no theaters or bars. U.S. and other foreign workers lived very comfortably, but in communities isolated from the Saudis.

King Faisal followed a policy of modernization in economic matters; he built sewage and water treatment plants, hospitals, and schools. He paved roads and built a strong air force with the latest planes. The conservative Moslem social order remained. Saudi homes had separate entrances for women, and women were not allowed to drive cars or ride alone in taxis. Punishments were traditional. After three convictions for theft, a hand was cut off; capital punishment was by beheading.

The full force of Saudi power could not be used against the United States because so many of the skilled oil workers were American, and the United States was their most powerful friend and protector. In 1979 some military officers attempted a coup against King Khalid that was put down. The Saudis signed an agreement with the United States to guarantee its independence under the present rulers. In return, Saudi Arabia increased oil production.

Israel was less of a threat to the Saudis than Moslem fanatics were. In 1979 fanatics seized control of the Grand Mosque at Mecca and held the worshippers hostage until the National Guard captured them. This problem increased when the Ayatollah Khomeini came to power in Iran.

KUWAIT was a small nation squeezed between Saudi Arabia and Iraq on the Persian Gulf. Independent since 1961, its greatest threat to survival was Iraq. Kuwait's oil had more sulphur than was normal, so it did not receive the highest prices. However, with the price of oil jumping in 1973, Kuwait's oil looked more attractive, and it became an important player in the oil business. In 1977 the government took over the foreign oil companies and made them part of the Kuwait Petroleum Corporation (KPC). The increased price of oil made it possible for Kuwait to create a welfare state with the government providing medical care, education, and even free drinking water.

IRAN had been ruled since 1941 by Shah Mohammed Reza Pahlavi. During World War II, British and Russian troops were sent there, and when the war ended, the Russians stayed until the United States and Great Britain pressured them to leave. Relations with Britain were bad because many Iranians resented the British-owned Anglo-Iranian Oil Company (AIOC). In 1951 Premier Mohammed Mossadegh nationalized the company against British opposition. In 1953 a coup aided by the United States and Britain overthrew him. A new arrangement followed whereby oil companies shared profits equally with Iran.

The Shah's program included land reform and modernizing the country, but without political freedom. When the price of oil rose in 1973, he had dreams of making Iran into a great world power, but progress led to high inflation, political protest, and the arrest of critics by SAVAK (the secret police). In 1964 he exiled the Ayatollah Khomeini, who went to Paris. Mass demonstrations broke out against the Shah in January 1979, and this time, nothing could stop them. In February, the Shah left Iran.

Discussion

1. How did the Arab oil embargo affect American life, both at the time and afterward?
2. In what ways is Saudi Arabia a modern country? Why does it keep so many of the old ways?
3. What are some reasons for Saudi Arabia and the United States to be friends? What are some problems that keep them from being "best friends"?

Name _____ Date _____

CHALLENGES

1. Of the five nations starting OPEC, which were Middle Eastern?

_____

_____

2. What was a normal price for gasoline in the United States before 1973? How much were Americans paying after the oil embargo? _____

_____

3. How much did oil cost in January 1973 and how much in January 1974? What was the difference in price-per-gallon? _____

_____

4. What caused OPEC to cut oil production in 1973?

_____

5. What nations ranked first, third, and fourth in oil reserves?

_____

6. What does Saudi Arabia do to discourage theft?

_____

7. What are the chances of being hit by a woman driver in Saudi Arabia? Why?

_____

8. What happened in 1979 that caused the Saudi government to become especially worried about fanatic extremists? _____

_____

9. What was Mossadegh's attitude toward the AIOC? What happened to him?

_____

_____

10. What was SAVAK, and what did it do for the Shah's popularity?

_____

_____

Map Activities

Using map A, locate and label Iran, Iraq, Kuwait, Saudi Arabia, Qatar, Bahrain, United Arab Emirates, and Oman. Also, locate and label the Persian Gulf, the Arabian Sea, and the Tigris and Euphrates Rivers. Also, locate and label Baghdad, Riyad, Tehran, Mecca, Abu Dhabi, and Doha. Using a pen or pencil of a different color, write OPEC on member states. Also, write the names Mossadegh, the Shah, Khomeini, and King Faisal on the country in which each lived.

KHOMEINI TAKES ON THE "GREAT SATAN"

A bitter old man sat in his Paris apartment scheming ways to get even with the Pahlavi family, which lived in wealth and decadence in Tehran while he lived in exile in a foreign land. Born in 1900, Khomeini was a Shiite Moslem with a hatred for the modernism that was eating away at the heart of Islam. A scholar of Islamic teachings, he was honored with the title of *ayatollah* (teacher) in the 1950s.

Ayatollah Ruhollah Khomeini

His often-expressed dislike for the Shah of Iran led to his imprisonment and in 1964 to his exile to Iraq. His further accusations against the Iranian ruler caused Iraq to expel him, and in 1978 he and his second wife were exiled to Paris. Now, his determination grew even stronger and so did his popularity as a leader.

Not only did Khomeini attack the Shah, but he also blamed the United States, which he called the "great Satan" for supporting the corrupt Shah and his puppets, who paid no taxes but spent millions on arms. The United States appreciated the Shah's help in supplying American oil needs, but made the mistake of ignoring the abuses by SAVAK (the Iranian secret police) and the growing rift between the Shah and his people. The United States blamed disturbances on a few religious zealots or the Communist Tudeh Party.

Khomeini sent taped messages into Iran that were broadcast to the country by religious backers. In October 1978 he called for a general strike, and that was followed the next month by strikes of oil field workers. The success of these efforts paralyzed the economy and made it clear that Khomeini had more power among the people than the Shah.

The Shah was forced to leave Iran in January 1979 and began drifting from one country to another. In February 1979 the Tudeh Party captured the U.S. embassy and held its personnel hostage; Khomeini ordered that they be freed, and they were set free immediately. Then the Shah came to the United States in October for cancer treatment. Khomeini was furious with President Carter for allowing the Shah to enter the country, and demonstrations outside the U.S. embassy in Tehran began. Again, mobs stormed the embassy, but this time, embassy personnel were captured with Khomeini's permission. Americans rallied around the hostages, and yellow ribbons were put around trees as a sign of support. The United States demanded that the embassy personnel be released.

Khomeini held no government titles, but it was clear that no Iranian official dared act in any way without his approval. Going through normal diplomatic channels did not work, and a frustrated President Carter tried a number of approaches in his efforts to get the Americans out. As soon as the Shah was healthy enough to travel, he was sent to Panama, where he died in 1980. The United States put an embargo on Iranian oil. Then, in April 1980, the United States sent helicopters into Iran to take the hostages out. Two helicopters went down in the Iranian desert during the failed rescue attempt.

In the meantime, all kinds of problems were breaking out in the region. The United States got involved in the struggle between rival leaders in Afghanistan when the American ambassador was kidnapped and killed. The Russians decided to take charge of the Afghan situation and moved troops in; the United States saw this as a clear sign of Russian imperialism and took several actions designed to punish the Soviets, including a grain embargo and refusal to send athletes to the 1980 Olympic games held in Moscow.

Iran was having its troubles as well. Inside the country, a struggle was going on for control of the government. Supporters of Khomeini formed the Islamic Republic Party (IRP), and it got control of the parliament and opposed the elected president, Bani-Sadr. The president lost the support of Khomeini and was impeached. Rising to oppose the IRP was the Mujahedin, who backed Massud Rajavi. Both sides used terror, and political murders and arrests became common.

Iran was now unpopular with both the United States and Russia and was torn by internal conflict. Saddam Hussein of Iraq decided this was a good time to push Iran back from oil fields along the border between the two nations. In September 1980 Iraq attacked, and for two years had the upper hand. The Iranians succeeded in taking back most of the lost territory by 1982, but Khomeini kept the war going in the hope of defeating Hussein.

The United States was engaged in a struggle for power as well—one far more peaceful. Carter won the Democratic nomination for a second term, but Ronald Reagan, the Republican challenger, won the 1980 presidential election by a large margin. Part of the reason for Carter's defeat was the failure of his policies toward Iran and Afghanistan. Reagan was no friendlier toward the Iranians than Carter. He called them "nothing better than criminals and kidnappers." Like Carter, he refused to consider paying any ransom for the return of the captives.

Both countries had good reason to see the issue settled. The last details of an arrangement were worked out in January 1981, and as Reagan was being inaugurated president, the Iranians released the hostages. Both nations had been hurt by the crisis. Iran had been damaged by the war with Iraq and the steps backward under strict Islamic rules. The United States suffered from the rise in the cost of oil and the loss of a stable and friendly government in Iran.

Discussion

1. Do you think Khomeini had some grounds for blaming the United States for the corruption and tyranny of the Shah's government?

2. Why did the taking of embassy personnel as hostages so anger Americans? If it happened at an embassy today, do you think the reaction would be the same?

3. Trouble in one country often spreads to its neighbors? What happened because of the turmoil in Iran?

4. Do you think there might have been some reason why Iran released the captives at the time they did?

5. Do you think the United States should try to develop friendly relations with Iran today?

Name _____ Date _____

CHALLENGES

1. Why was Khomeini in Paris?

_____

_____

2. What particular person did he hate most?

_____

3. Why did he call the United States the "Great Satan"?

_____

4. Whom did the United States think was behind the anti-Shah movement?

_____

5. Why did President Carter allow the Shah to enter the United States?

_____

6. What happened in Tehran because of it?

_____

_____

7. How did Americans show their support for the hostages?

_____

8. What were two actions by the United States against Russia that were caused by the Russian invasion of Afghanistan? _____

_____

_____

9. Who took advantage of the trouble between the United States and Iran?

_____

10. What did Reagan think of the Iranians?

_____

Map Activity

    Using Map A, locate and label Iran, Iraq, Afghanistan, Turkey, Kuwait, Jordan, Syria, Lebanon, Israel, Saudi Arabia, and the former Soviet Union. Also locate and label the Tigris and Euphrates Rivers, the Mediterranean Sea, the Red Sea, the Black Sea, the Caspian Sea, and the Persian Gulf. Using a pen or pencil of a different color, locate and label Baghdad and Tehran. Also write the names Khomeini and Saddam Hussein on the country in which they lived or live.

SADDAM HUSSEIN AND THE DESERT STORM

Saddam Hussein

In 1991 Americans sat glued to their television sets as they watched an amazing display of fireworks in the Middle East. The world's attention focused on Saddam Hussein, the ruler of Iraq, who vowed that if the United States tried to stop him, he would create the "mother of battles." Hussein's record was one of plots and intrigues, murders, betrayals, and self-glorification. His name, Saddam, means "one who confronts." He had confronted the Iranians in a war that had killed thousands on both sides. He had confronted the Kurds, who wanted independence, and killed thousands of them with chemical weapons. With the fourth largest army in the world (a million men in uniform), he confidently predicted that Iraq could beat any combination of countries that might oppose him.

Despite his "bad guy" image in the rest of the world, Iraqis saw Hussein as a bold leader who took care of his people, and in the slums of the Middle East, he was the one who stood up against the Western imperialists. His oil money went not only into the military, but into food and education programs; Iraq's literacy rate is the highest in the region. He was popular, but feared. His secret police punished any who opposed him. He shot opponents and required cabinet members to execute traitors, as well.

In July 1990 Hussein started threatening Kuwait, Iraq's small neighbor to the south and east. He had long resented the wealth of Kuwait and the rich lifestyle of its people. With a small population and prosperity, Kuwaitis lived in ease, with the government providing everything from education through college to free drinking water for its people. He charged that Kuwait was (1) really a province of Iraq, (2) was illegally stealing oil from the Iraqi Rumaili oil field, (3) had over-produced oil beyond its OPEC limits, and (4) had lent millions to Iraq during the Iraq-Iran conflict and had the nerve to want it paid back. Hussein said Kuwait's systematic, deliberate, and contemptuous actions amounted to military aggression.

On August 1, 1990, Iraq invaded Kuwait, and many Kuwaitis, including the royal family, fled the country. Those remaining behind suffered brutal treatment at the hands of the Iraqis. The United States demanded Iraq's withdrawal. An Iraqi diplomat predicted that the United States and Iraq would go to war, and "America will lose and America will be humiliated."

British Prime Minister Margaret Thatcher advised President Bush to build a coalition of nations to force Iraq out. By the time war began, 28 nations had sent 698,000 troops. Even Egypt and Syria sent troops. West Germany and Japan sent no troops, but gave much needed financial support to the coalition. Russia cooperated by stopping arms shipments to Iraq and tried to persuade Iraq to withdraw. Saddam Hussein stubbornly refused.

Leading coalition forces was U.S. General Norman Schwarzkopf, who had support from General Colin Powell (chairman of the U.S. Joint Chiefs of Staff) and U.S. Secretary of Defense Dick Cheney, in assembling the operation. The weapons facing Iraq included the new Tomahawk missiles and the older Patriot missiles (able to blow up Scud missiles in the air). Ground forces were supported by the Abrams tanks. A variety of aircraft were used: Stealth fighters (not visible on radar screens), B-52s, F-11s, Apache helicopters, and others. Naval power included the *U.S.S. Missouri* to soften Iraqi positions along the coast, aircraft carriers, and support ships.

On November 29, 1990, the United Nations warned Iraq that it had to be out of Kuwait by January 15, 1991, and return all American and British hostages it held. Talks by the United States and Russia with Iraq were futile. On January 13 Iraq made it clear that it had no intention of giving in. Hussein warned this would be the "mother of all wars" and thousands of Americans would die.

On January 16 air attacks on Iraq began, and within days, most of the Iraqi air force was destroyed; to save his best 142 planes, Hussein sent them to neutral Iran, which did not return them until after the war was over. Baghdad and other Iraqi cities were defenseless against the air attacks, since their radar installations had been the first targets of the Stealths. Some effort was made by Russia to convince Hussein to quit, but he refused to give a date for withdrawal from Kuwait.

Saddam Hussein hoped that if he could provoke Israel to attack Iraq, Arab members of the coalition might withdraw. Scuds were aimed at Tel Aviv, and some hit in the city, but the United States persuaded Israel not to strike back. Patriot missile teams were sent to Israel. The only Arab country giving Iraq any real support was Jordan.

The ground war broke out Sunday, February 24; the "mother of all battles" was over in 100 hours. Morale of Iraqi troops broke quickly, and large units raised the white flag of surrender. With Kuwait about to be lost, Iraqis set fire to oil rigs, creating a blanket of thick smoke over the country. Kuwait City was recaptured February 27, and a conditional cease fire was signed the next day. Iraq agreed to give up any claim to Kuwait, surrender its prisoners, and return all stolen property.

The war ended with Hussein still in power. Within a few weeks, he was his old, defiant self, refusing to let the United Nations into factories believed to be capable of producing chemical and atomic weapons. U.N. resolutions and economic sanctions seemed only to make Hussein more defiant.

Discussion

1. Comparing the way the Gulf War began with the way World War II started, do you think Hussein's mistakes resembled Hitler's?
2. Hussein had a strong army and air force on paper. What did his army lack that the coalition had?
3. Why do you think Iran decided to stay neutral?
4. After the war, there was much debate over whether President Bush should have allowed coalition armies to capture Baghdad and carry Hussein away as a prisoner. The president argued that such an attack might destroy the coalition. Which side was right?

Name _____ Date _____

CHALLENGES

1. What does Saddam mean in Arabic?

_____

2. What group in Iraq had Hussein used chemical weapons against?

_____

3. Why was Hussein so admired in the Arab world?

_____

4. What did Hussein resent about the Kuwaitis?

_____

_____

5. What was Iraq's reaction to U.S. threats?

_____

_____

6. Who commanded the coalition forces?

_____

7. What were three missiles used in the war?

_____

8. What did Hussein do to protect his best planes?

_____

9. How did Hussein hope to provoke Israel into entering the war, thereby splitting the coalition? _____

_____

10. How long did it take for the land war to last before Iraq was ready to ask for peace?

_____

Map Activity

   Using Map A, locate and label Iran, Iraq, Egypt, Turkey, Kuwait, Jordan, Syria, Lebanon, Israel, Saudi Arabia, Qatar, the United Arab Emirates, and Russia. Also locate and lable the Tigris and Euphrates Rivers, the Nile River, the Mediterranean Sea, the Red Sea, the Black Sea, the Caspian Sea, the Persian Gulf, the Strait of Hormuz, the Sinai Peninsula, and the Gaza Strip. Using a pen or pencil of a different color, locate and label Baghdad, Tehran, Amman, Tel Aviv, Kuwait City, Riyadh, and Bahrain. Using still another color, locate, label, and lightly shade in the area known as Kurdistan, which includes southern Turkey, northern Iraq, and the east central portion of Iran.

THE PLO AND ISRAEL: CAN THEY LIVE IN PEACE?

In 1968 the Palestine Liberation Organization (PLO) drafted its charter. It said: "Armed struggle is the only way to liberate Palestine. Thus it is the overall strategy, not merely a tactical phase." The strategy was to fight until victory was won, the Zionists (Jews) were ousted, and the land returned to Arabs. Stated in lines from a Western movie: "It's either us or them, but there will be no peace in the valley until one of us is dead."

In 1969 Yasir Arafat became the leader of the PLO. An Egyptian by birth, he was trained as an engineer and as a demolition expert by Egypt's army. He became leader of *al-Fatah* (a group determined to drive the Israelis from Palestine) in 1964. *Al-Fatah* was more militant than the original PLO, and Israel saw him as a definite threat.

PLO leader Yasir Arafat

Surrounded by Arabs and with Arabs living in their land, Israel's Jews faced serious questions, especially after the 1973 war. By seizing the West Bank, they added one million Arabs to their population.

The Israelis could have tried moving them off the land, but that was not possible. Instead, they gave the West Bank the right to hold elections. The men elected were more radical than the Israelis wanted; instead of calming the Palestinians down, stone-throwing and terrorist incidents occurred. The PLO blamed trigger-happy Israeli soldiers; the Israelis blamed troublemakers stirred up by Israel's enemies: Iraq, Syria, and Egypt.

In 1977 the United States had a new president, Jimmy Carter, and Monachem Begin became Israel's prime minister. Carter reasoned that Secretary of State Henry Kissinger's work in the Nixon-Ford years had made some kind of agreement possible. President Anwar Sadat of Egypt wanted the Sinai Peninsula back, and Begin wanted recognition by a major Arab state. In November 1977 Sadat went to Israel and offered peace in return for Israel giving up the Sinai desert, taken in 1967. The next year, Carter invited Sadat and Begin to Camp David, and for days the leaders met to work out a "framework for peace." There were many details, and at times, the conversations were heated. The final treaty was signed in 1979. Israel was to pull back from the Sinai in three stages, and trade and diplomatic relations would begin the next year.

Egypt and Israel were happy, but the Palestinians were not. They felt that Sadat had ignored their needs completely. PLO raids out of Lebanon increased. At times, Israel's air force bombed Palestinian bases, or its army crossed the line to punish them.

Everyone was becoming short-tempered. The new Reagan administration in the United States blamed Israel for stirring up trouble with the Arabs by attacking Lebanon and bombing Beirut. Israel blamed the PLO. Lebanon's government was too weak to prevent the Palestinians, Syrians, or Israelis from doing whatever they chose. U.S. officials had no idea which way to go.

Only young Palestinians seemed to know what they wanted. They were fed up with the PLO, which they felt had done nothing for them; but even more, they saw the Israelis as colonial rulers who denied them a homeland and jobs. They called their movement the *Intifada* or "shaking off." They struck back at the Israeli army that shot and tear-gassed them, but their special anger was directed toward Israelis building settlements on the West Bank. Settlers and Intifada traded terrorist acts against each other and created a political crisis for Israel. Israel's two major political parties disagreed on how to handle the situation. The Labor Party favored trading land for peace. The Likud Party wanted large-scale settlement. Israel's public was about evenly divided on the issue.

American Middle East concerns moved in different directions. The Reagan administration attacked Libya's Muammar Qaddafi for supporting terrorism, and U.S.–Iraqi relations turned sour in 1987 after two Iraqi missiles hit an American destroyer. Then, the Gulf War came, and U.S. prestige in the Middle East rose to a new high. Meanwhile, Russian influence declined.

Arafat was in trouble. He had backed Iraq in the war, could no longer expect financial support from Russia, and had angered the Saudis and the other Arab states that fought Iraq. Inside the PLO, a more radical *Hamas* faction was growing. Arafat had no choice except to talk with Israel.

In 1991 Secretary of State Jim Baker set up a Middle East peace conference held at Madrid in 1992. Israel was not enthused, but President Bush twisted their arm by holding back $10 billion in loan guarantees. Israeli elections in 1992 brought the Labor Party back into power. The new leaders, Yitzhak Rabin and Shimon Peres worked with the PLO on a plan for self-rule for Palestinians in the Gaza Strip and the West Bank. Many Israelis and Arabs, however, are determined to prevent peace at all costs: terrorist acts have been committed to bring reprisals. While political leaders debate, homes for Israelis are being built. Anger with Arafat is growing among Palestinians.

From its earliest times, the Middle East has faced difficulties between nations. The winds of the desert blow in many directions, and few can predict where the sands will finally rest. Wise and courageous Middle Eastern statesmen must resolve the region's issues. The United States and other outsiders can help the negotiating process along, but cannot bring it peace.

Discussion

1. If you were an Israeli, do you think the charter of the PLO would make you nervous about any dealings with them?
2. Why don't the Israelis hold elections for the Knesset that include all Palestinians?
3. If the Palestinian issue had been taken up at Camp David, do you think any agreement could have been made?
4. If you were Israeli, would you join the Likud or the Labor Party? Why?

Name _____ Date _____

CHALLENGES

1. What group did Yasir Arafat head in 1964? What did it want?

_____

2. How did conquering the West Bank add to Israel's problems?

_____

_____

3. What happened when Israel held elections on the West Bank?

_____

_____

4. What nations did Israel feel were behind stone-throwing incidents?

_____

5. Who were the three leaders meeting at Camp David?

_____

6. According to the agreement (the Camp David Accords), what was to happen in the Sinai desert? _____

_____

7. How did the PLO feel about the Camp David Accords?

_____

8. Which group in Israel did *Intifada* especially dislike?

_____

9. What mistake had Arafat made during the Gulf War?

_____

10. What Israeli leaders worked with the PLO on self-rule for the Palestinians?

_____

Map Activity

Using Map A, locate and label Egypt, Israel, the West Bank, the Gaza Strip, Iran, Iraq, Turkey, Kuwait, Jordan, Syria, Lebanon, Saudi Arabia, Libya, and Russia. Also locate and label the Tigris and Euphrates Rivers, the Nile River, the Mediterranean Sea, the Red Sea, the Gulf of Aqaba, the Gulf of Suez, the Black Sea, the Caspian Sea, the Persian Gulf, and the Sinai Peninsula. Using a pen or pencil of a different color, locate and label Tel Aviv, Jerusalem, Beirut, Cairo, Baghdad, Amman, and Damascus. Using still another color, locate, label, and lightly shade in the area known as Palestine in ancient times, which included the area of modern Israel and the area owned by Jordan located on the west bank of the Jordan River. Also place these names on the countries in which they lived or live: Monachem Begin, Anwar Sadat, Muammar Qaddafi, Yasir Arafat, Yitzhak Rabin, and Shimon Peres.

102

MAP A

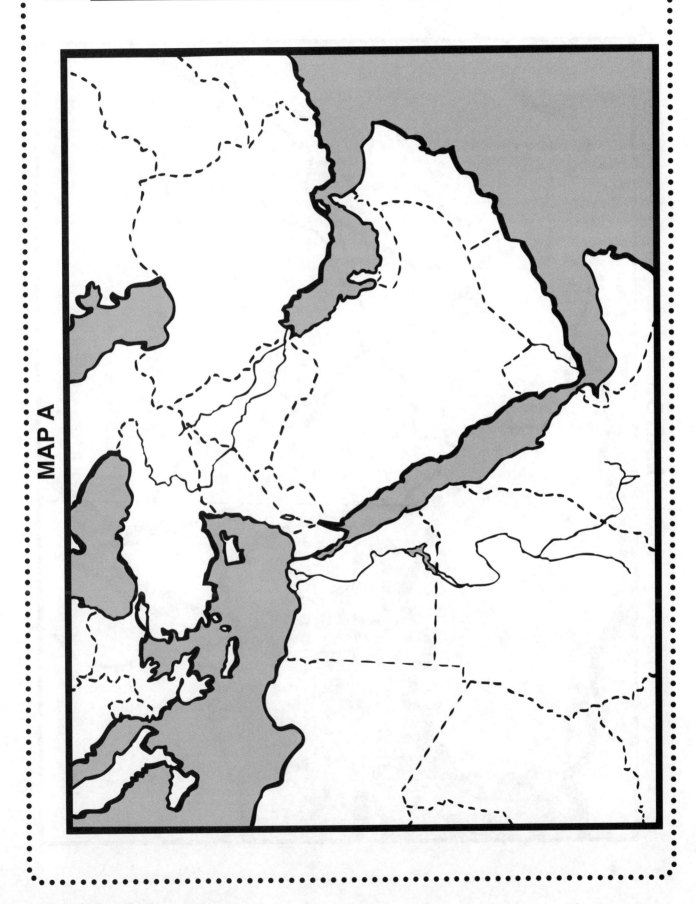

Name _____ Date _____

MAP B

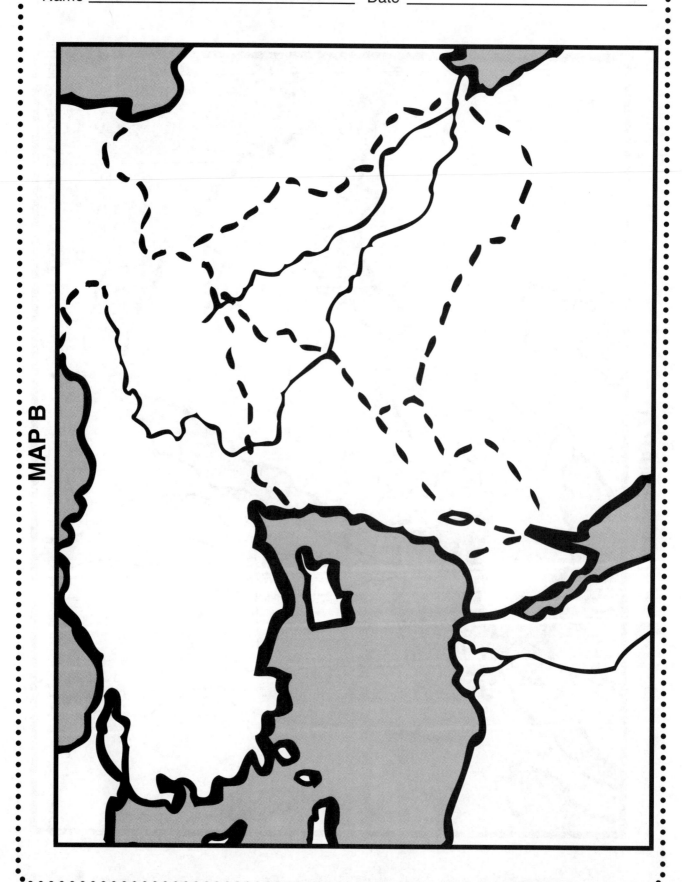

104

Name _____   Date _____

MAP C

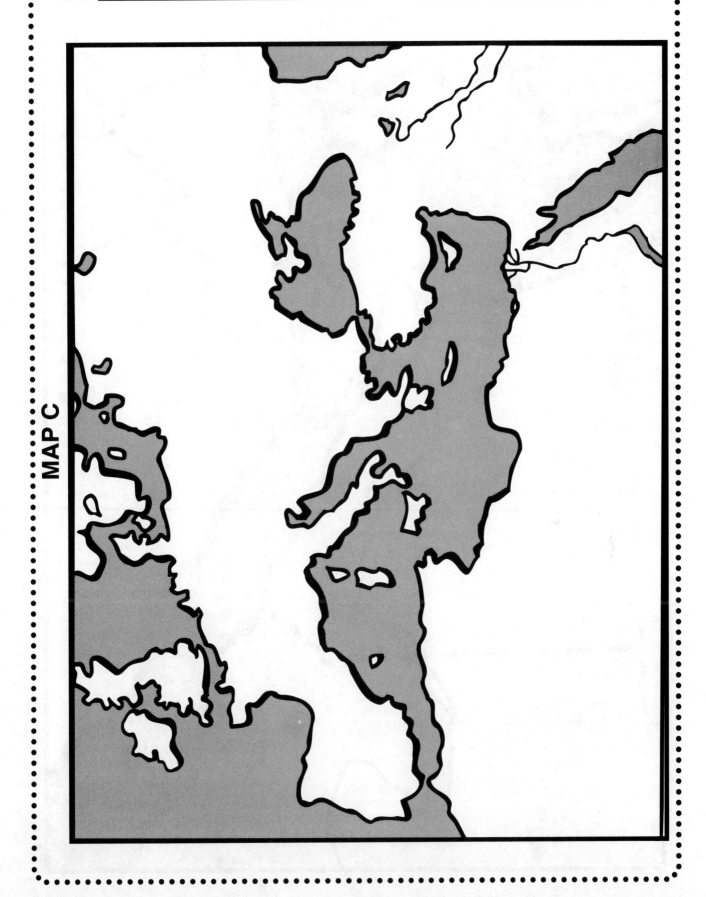

Name _____ Date _____

MAP D

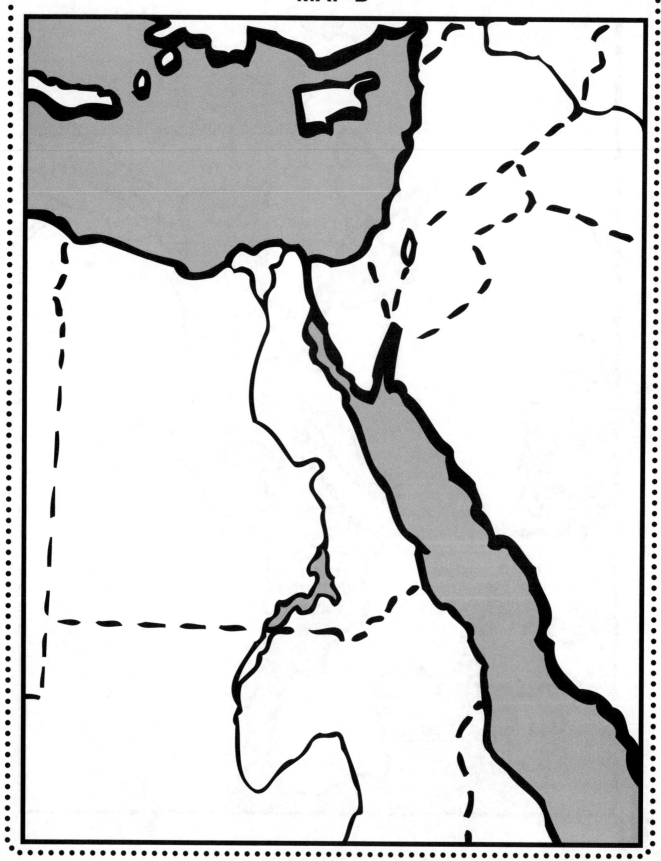

Name _____ Date _____

CROSSWORD PUZZLE

Use the clues below to complete the puzzle. Answers to the clues may be found in the narrative pages.

ACROSS

4. The first known author in history
6. _____ collected almost 300 rulings to establish a law code for the Babylonians.
7. The area in which the first civilization formed
11. First pharaoh of the united Egypt
13. Middle Eastern nation ranked #1 in oil reserves (two words)
14. People who split into two kingdoms after King Solomon died
15. Loyal slaves of the Ottoman sultan who made up an elite infantry corps

DOWN

1. The founder of the Persian Empire
2. The Phoenicians lived in what is known as _____ today.
3. Antony faced the Roman navy at the Battle of __.
5. New capital built during the reign of Akhenaton
6. Woman who ruled as pharaoh
7. The founder of Islam
8. Those the Crusaders wished to drive from the Holy Land (two words)
9. Group led by Yasir Arafat
10. Leader of Iraq who faced the United States in the Gulf War (two words)
11. Egyptians depended on the regularity of the ___ River.
12. According to the prophecy of the Gordian Knot, he was destined to be lord of all Asia.

Name _____ Date _____

MATCHING

Match the terms in Column B with the correct statements in Column A.

COLUMN A	**COLUMN B**
_____ 1. "new stone age"	A. Amon-Re
_____ 2. Wedge-shaped, Sumerian writing	B. Balfour Declaration
_____ 3. Sumerian temple	C. Christianity
_____ 4. Sumerian "big man" or king	D. Cuneiform
_____ 5. An upright stone slab with a relief picture carved into it	E. Devshirme
_____ 6. Order, justice, and truth	F. Diaspora
_____ 7. The name for the soul in Egyptian religion	G. Hellenistic
_____ 8. The god who brought civilization to Egypt	H. Hieroglyphics
_____ 9. The Egyptian Sun god	I. Hittites
_____ 10. The writing of the Egyptians that used pictures	J. Hyksos
_____ 11. The first invaders to conquer Egypt who came with chain mail, compound bows, and horse-drawn chariots	K. Jihad
	L. Ka
	M. Knesset
_____ 12. Enemies of the Egyptians who had three-man chariots	N. Koran
_____ 13. The tendency to combine contradictory beliefs	O. Lugal
_____ 14. One who worships only one god	P. Ma'at
_____ 15. The founder of Assyrian religion	Q. Monotheist
_____ 16. The exile of the Jews from Palestine	R. Nationalism
_____ 17. Civilization that mixed ideas from Greece with those of the Middle East	S. Neolithic
	T. Osiris
_____ 18. This eventually became the religion of the Roman Empire	U. Ramadan
	V. Stele
_____ 19. The sacred book of Islam	W. Syncretism
_____ 20. The Islamic month of fasting	X. Ziggurat
_____ 21. The "boy tax" imposed by the Ottoman sultan	Y. Zoroaster
_____ 22. The belief that a group of people who share the same language and culture should form an independent state	
_____ 23. An Islamic holy war	
_____ 24. Statement by the British cabinet approving a Jewish homeland	
_____ 25. The Israeli legislature	

ANSWER KEYS

Landing in the Middle East (page 3)
1. An area striped with green shaped like a fan
2. Egypt, Syria, Jordan, Lebanon, Israel, Iran, Iraq, Saudi Arabia, Kuwait, Bahrain, Qatar, The Untied Arab Emirates, Oman, South Yemen, Yemen, Sudan, and Turkey
3. Libya, Algeria, Morocco, Afghanistan, Turkistan, and Pakistan
4. Washington or New York
5. There was a constant flow of peoples, tribes, armies, merchants, and pilgrims.
6. The size of the continental United States
7. Irrigation
8. Technology and new ways of organizing people were discovered as the inhabitants came up with answers to the problems of irrigation.
9. The Nile, Tigris, and Euphrates Rivers
10. It runs from the Nile Valley up along the eastern coast of the Mediterranean around the northern edge of the Syrian Desert and down the Euphrates River Valley.

Bones from the Distant Past: The Neolithic Revolution (page 6)
1. New stone age
2. Sometime before 10,000 B.C.
3. It was a change in the way of life of early man from hunting and gathering to settled agriculture in villages.
4. Wheat and barley
5. They could store food for later use.
6. Civilization
7. Jericho
8. In many places at the same time
9. Either for defense against invaders or floods

The Dawn of Civilization (page 9)
1. Evidence of a hierarchy, formal political and religious institutions, monumental architecture, and writing
2. 3500 and 3000 B.C.; in Mesopotamia
3. The challenge of living in the harsh environment of dry, hot summers and unpredictable flooding
4. Specialists were needed to plan and supervise the engineering projects and study the stars to predict the yearly floods.
5. Wheel, plow, bronze, dates, figs, and olives
6. Melted copper and mixed it with tin
7. ca. 3000 B.C.
8. Used tiny clay tokens to represent objects being counted or traded
9. Simplified pictures that stand for a particular object
10. Writing symbols in wet clay tablets with a reed stylus shaped like a triangle

The Stairway to Heaven: Ancient Sumer (page 12)
1. The belief in many gods
2. Gods who looked and acted like humans
3. The ziggurat was built in the form of seven ascending terraces with a temple on top.
4. The invention of the potter's wheel
5. Dates, flax, wheat, barley, and possibly grapes
6. Ur; 4,500 years old
7. Approximately 12
8. The limited water supply offered by the Tigris and Euphrates Rivers
9. Oman, Sinai, Armenia, and Nubia
10. In the third millennium B.C., or around 2500 B.C.

Sargon the Conqueror: The Rise of Kings (page 15)
1. Through his own efforts
2. The people of all lands or the four corners of the earth
3. He controlled all of the Sumerian city-states.
4. He penetrated Anatolia and went down the Euphrates River to the Persian Gulf.
5. He took the name Sargon, which means "the king is legitimate."
6. Enheduanna
7. They are flat surfaces with images or figures projecting up from the surface.
8. Over 100 years.
9. It strengthened the bonds between cities.
10. It spread Sumerian culture to neighboring peoples.

Gilgamesh Battles with Death: The Gods of Ancient Sumer (page 18)
1. Noah's ark, the Garden of Eden, Job
2. They lived in a harsh environment of little rain, unpredictable rivers, and constant warfare.
3. A story of heroic deeds usually written in the form of a long poem
4. They were conquerors of Mesopotamia.
5. 60
6. They believed that by studying the movement of the stars, they could predict the future.
7. Hammurabi's Code
8. Slaves, free people who owned land, and others who were free but worked for the land owners
9. They could own and inherit property and testify in court.
10. The culprit would lose his eye, too.

The Gift of the Nile: The Rise of Ancient Egypt (page 21)
1. Southern Egypt
2. By the conquest of King Narmer
3. Old, Middle, and New Kingdom
4. Because Egypt was dependent upon the Nile River for almost everything
5. Its flooding is predictable.
6. Because Egypt is protected by deserts on both sides and has an abundance of water
7. Because the Nile brought new life every year to Egypt

8. They relied on it to bring new soil and water.
9. The stability of life
10. A day in the life of an Egyptian during the reign of Narmer was very similar to a day in the life of an Egyptian 3,000 years later.

The Glories of Egypt: The Pyramids and the Sphinx (page 24)
1. The experts didn't want more competition for work.
2. From death to burial took 70 days.
3. The soul
4. Men and sandstorms have caused deterioration.
5. A tomb for the pharaoh's officials
6. The principle of order, justice, and truth
7. Gizeh, near ancient Memphis in Egypt
8. Herodotus estimated 100,000 men and 20 years.
9. They used water trenches.
10. The Pyramid Texts guided the pharaoh through the underworld to the Sun god.

The Eye of Horus: The Egyptian Gods (page 27)
1. The god who brought civilization to Egypt
2. Osiris's evil brother who was god of storms, chaos, and the desert
3. It either began with Isis's tears or it flowed from Osiris's body.
4. The lost eye of Horus
5. The tendency to combine contradictory beliefs
6. The sky is sometimes portrayed as the goddess Nut, and at other times it is portrayed as a cow.
7. Horus was portrayed as a falcon.
8. Over 2,000
9. He was one of the gods of sun, earth, and water and took the shape of a crocodile.
10. He was the architect of the first pyramid.

Grave Robbers: The End of the Old Kingdom (page 30)
1. Provincial governors
2. He reunified Egypt after the First Intermediate Period.
3. 2040 B.C.
4. Their construction exhausted the resources of the state.
5. When they slackened, the Nile dried up.
6. Anarchy, with brother fighting brother, cannibalism, government files thrown into the streets, and Egypt divided
7. Thebes
8. They began to make their sons co-rulers so that they could gain experience ruling and be sure that no one would challenge their right to rule when the old pharaoh died.
9. Pharaohs are portrayed as concerned and even worried.
10. They were inward-looking and serious and interested in a sense of common humanity and ethics.

The Test of the Afterlife: The Middle Kingdom (page 33)
1. Ma'at
2. Thoth
3. It came from weaving fibers of the papyrus plant that grew along the Nile.
4. By drawing pictures
5. 600
6. D
7. Scribes
8. From father to son
9. Papyrus scrolls containing prayers, spells, historical records, poetry, technical treatises in mathematics and medicine, wisdom stories, letters, business contracts, and royal proclamations
10. Because papyrus used for many kinds of writing survived in Egyptian tombs

The War Chariots of the Hyksos: The End of the Middle Kingdom (page 36)
1. Located on the east coast of Africa probably near Somalia
2. Gold
3. Cedar logs
4. It was a sign of status.
5. Long pleated fabric, heavy bracelets and necklaces made of gold
6. Malachite and red ocher
7. As a place to store water
8. The horse-drawn chariot
9. Hyksos
10. The Second Intermediate Period

The Warrior Pharaohs of the New Kingdom (page 39)
1. The gold of Valor and slaves
2. The Hyksos
3. The horse-drawn chariot
4. Syria and Palestine
5. The Hittites
6. Kadesh
7. They had bigger chariots.
8. Building
9. Abu Simbel
10. Because it was threatened by the construction of Aswan High Dam

Queen Hatshepsut: The Woman Who Was Pharaoh (page 42)
1. Thutmose III
2. She ruled as pharaoh instead of her son.
3. It is open to the sun.
4. She built a hidden tomb in the Valley of the Kings.
5. Senmut
6. Because he secretly sneaked carvings of himself into her temple

7. She renewed foreign commerce.
8. Myrrh trees, ebony, ivory, gold, eye cosmetics, giraffes, hippopotami, apes, monkeys, and greyhounds
9. 20 years
10. Because Egyptian law said that women could not be pharaohs

Akhenaton the Bizarre (page 45)
1. Either he was deformed because of a glandular disorder, or he wanted to emphasize his closeness with a creator god.
2. The priests of Amon-Re
3. Because they were rich and powerful
4. Aton
5. Akhenaton
6. The Amarna period
7. More realistic art forms
8. Akhenaton's wife
9. The priests of Amon-Re re-established control.
10. The Hittites overran the Egyptian possessions in Syria and Palestine.

The Tomb of Tutankhamen (page 48)
1. The Valley of the Kings
2. 1922 by Howard Carter
3. It had not been robbed.
4. 9 years
5. The worship of Aton was abolished, and Akhenaton's city was abandoned.
6. He reconquered Palestine and Syria.
7. He built the largest Egyptian temple at Karnak.
8. The cost of maintaining a huge army, building monumental temples, and keeping the priests of Amon-Re content
9. By the end of Ramses III's reign
10. The Libyans, Nubians, and Assyrians

The Rise and Fall of Empires in the Middle East (page 51)
1. To pull the heavy three-man chariots
2. Manuals on horse care survive.
3. Most of the Middle East except Egypt
4. Hattusa
5. The kings ruled through a humane law code.
6. By terror
7. Nineveh
8. Persia
9. Cyrus
10. By leading a moral life based on truth

The Creative Nations of Phoenicia and Israel (page 54)
1. Because their land was trapped between the mountains and the sea
2. They could weather storms, yet carry plenty of cargo.
3. Throughout the Middle East, North Africa, and the coasts of Europe
4. Phoinix
5. An alphabet
6. They developed a monotheistic religion.
7. It was a way to understand God's actions.
8. Israel and Judah
9. A temple at Jerusalem, a palace, and fortresses
10. When the Hebrews were marched off to Babylon

Alexander the Great Conquers His World (page 57)
1. He who could untie it would be lord of all Asia.
2. He cut it.
3. He took advantage of divisions between the city-states of Greece.
4. 20
5. He built a causeway of stones as a bridge so his men could attack it.
6. Alexandria
7. By a mass wedding between Persians and Macedonians
8. 33
9. It mixed ideas from Greece with those found from Egypt to India.
10. His generals fought for control of it.

The Middle East and the Roman Empire (page 60)
1. They committed suicide.
2. Because they were fighting among themselves
3. They were a dutiful, disciplined, and practical people who excelled in the art of government.
4. Because the Romans promised security, efficient armed forces, and stability
5. Several centuries of peace enjoyed under Roman control
6. The city was taken and destroyed.
7. They committed suicide.
8. The surviving foundation of the Temple
9. The long period of exile of the Jews from Palestine
10. Spain

Christianity Conquers Rome (page 63)
1. The Essenes
2. The Gospels or the first four books of the New Testament (Matthew, Mark, Luke, John)
3. Because crowds were proclaiming him king or messiah, they feared that the Romans would see this as a sign of revolt.
4. Paul
5. A fire that burned most of Rome
6. Constantine

7. Diocletian
8. Constantinople
9. Most of the Middle East and North Africa
10. Byzantine

From the Sands of Arabia Comes Islam (page 66)
1. A.D. 610
2. The *Koran*
3. Those who follow the way of life laid out in the *Koran*
4. Those who submit to God
5. Shahadah, which means asserting there is no god but God and Mohammed is his messenger
6. Salat, which means bathing and prayer five times a day and at noon on Friday
7. Sawm, which means fasting during the month of Ramadan
8. Zakat, which means giving a part of one's income to the poor
9. Hajj, which means pilgrimage to Mecca at least once in one's life
10. Islam spread throughout the Middle East.

The Islamic Golden Age (page 69)
1. From all over the Middle East
2. The Caliph in Baghdad
3. A brilliant general who spread Islam
4. A splinter group that had grown up within Christianity
5. Byzantium and Persia
6. Because all trade routes between Europe, Asia, and Africa passed through the Middle East
7. A Persian physician who set bones with plaster casts and accurately described the symptoms of smallpox and measles
8. He was a Spanish-born scholar who revolutionized geography by creating spherical-shaped maps of the earth.
9. Because Islam forbade pictures or statues of natural objects
10. Spain

Crusaders Descend upon the Middle East (page 72)
1. By massacring most of Jerusalem's inhabitants
2. Alexius Comnenus I
3. An aggressive tribe from Central Asia
4. The visiting of holy places
5. Urban II
6. They were so badly organized that they had to prey on fellow Christians for food. They were attacked in Bulgaria and many were killed.
7. He lead an organized army.
8. Saladin
9. The Fourth Crusade
10. They were able to explore the coasts of Africa, Asia, and the Americas.

The Middle East Under the Power of the Turks (page 75)
1. The boy tax
2. The Mongols
3. Osman
4. Suleiman the Magnificent
5. Specially trained warrior-slaves
6. Istanbul
7. The European discoveries of new trade routes around the coast of Africa and across the Atlantic
8. Selim the Drunkard
9. They assassinated sultans who tried to initiate reforms.
10. The Middle East had fallen behind.

New Forces for Change in the Ottoman Empire (page 78)
1. Almost all of the shore of the Black Sea including the Crimean Peninsula
2. It impressed upon them the superior technology of the European powers.
3. It enabled archaeologists to decipher Egyptian hieroglyphics.
4. The Official Gazette of Muhammad Ali
5. In Greece and the Balkans
6. Russia, England, France, Sardinia, and the Ottoman Empire
7. A program of reforms launched by the Sultan Abdul Aziz and Ali Pasha
8. A group of reformers who seized power from Abdulhamid II
9. They tried to bring the Ottoman Empire into the 20th century.
10. Abdulhamid II

World War I and the Middle East (page 81)
1. Bismarck feared it would cause trouble with Russia.
2. Russia feared it might block their entrance to the Black Sea.
3. Pasha wanted German help to take part of Caucasus.
4. England needed them for the war.
5. Gallipoli fever was enthusiasm over attacking Gallipoli.
6. The navy needed oil for its ships.
7. T. E. Lawrence
8. Lawrence felt England was not protecting the Arabs.
9. Great Britain
10. Russia

The Mandate System (page 84)
1. No, it might favor the colonial power.
2. Yes, because it should give you self-rule.
3. Lloyd George
4. A foreign government would rule the country.
5. Ended polygamy, no longer required to wear veil, could go to school
6. Foreign policy
7. Lebanon

8. Great Britain; because of oil
9. Ataturk; They both tried to modernize their country.
10. Trade with tourists going to holy cities.

The Middle East and World War II (page 87)
1. El Alamein and Stalingrad
2. He was too pro-British.
3. They tried to free the country from British influence.
4. The flow of tourists had dropped.
5. Arabian-American Oil Company (ARAMCO)
6. The Tudeh
7. It was the best route for the allies to send aid to Russia.
8. Jews; It established a Jewish homeland in Palestine, which was already settled by Arabs.
9. In order to ensure the Arabs would continue to sell them oil
10. Terror organizations

Israel: The New Kid on the Block (page 90)
1. Haganah
2. Many left country
3. David Ben-Gurion
4. Legislature: Knesset; party: Mapai
5. For electricity and flood control
6. Israel, Great Britain, and France
7. Syria united with Egypt. The new nation was called the United Arab Republic.
8. Kurds; Turkey and Iran
9. The Golan Heights, West Bank, and Sinai desert
10. The PLO was driven out because they were a threat to King Hussein.

Oil Brings Changes to the Middle East (page 93)
1. Iran, Iraq, Saudi Arabia, and Kuwait
2. Prices: before 1973, 26 cents a gallon; after 1973, 40–50 cents a gallon
3. Prices: $2.74 and $11.65 per barrel. Per gallon: 4.98 cents a gallon in 1973; 21.18 cents a gallon in 1974
4. U.S. aid to Israel
5. Saudi Arabia, Iran, and Kuwait
6. After third conviction they cut off the thief's hand.
7. None, women can't drive.
8. Fanatics captured the Grand Mosque at Mecca.
9. Mossadegh wanted to nationalize it. He was overthrown.
10. SAVAK was the Iranian secret police. It hurt the Shah's popularity.

Khomeini Takes on the "Great Satan" (page 96)
1. He was exiled there by Iran and Iraq.
2. The Shah of Iran
3. The United States was supporting the Shah's regime.

4. The United States thought it was a few religious zealots and the Communist Tudeh Party.
5. For cancer treatments
6. Fundamentalists took over the U.S. embassy and held personnel hostage.
7. They tied yellow ribbons around trees.
8. The United States boycotted Moscow Olympics and stopped grain shipments.
9. Saddam Hussein of Iraq
10. Reagan called them "criminals and kidnappers."

Saddam Hussein and the Desert Storm (page 99)
1. "One who confronts"
2. Kurds
3. He stood up to the West.
4. He resented their rich lifestyle.
5. They believed that in case of war, Iraq would easily win.
6. Norman Schwarzkopf
7. Tomahawks, Patriots, and Scuds
8. He sent them to Iran.
9. By sending Scuds against Tel Aviv
10. 100 hours

The PLO and Israel: Can They Live in Peace? (page 102)
1. Al Fatah; It wanted to drive Israel from Palestine.
2. Added 1 million more Arabs
3. Those elected were radical.
4. Iraq, Syria, and Egypt
5. Carter, Begin, and Sadat
6. Israel was to withdraw in three stages.
7. The PLO was angry; it felt their interests were ignored.
8. Jewish settlers on the West Bank
9. He had supported Iraq.
10. Yitzhak Rabin and Shimon Peres

Crossword Puzzle (page 107)

Matching (page 108)

1. S	14. Q
2. D	15. Y
3. X	16. F
4. O	17. G
5. V	18. C
6. P	19. N
7. L	20. U
8. T	21. E
9. A	22. R
10. H	23. K
11. J	24. B
12. I	25. M
13. W	

BIBLIOGRAPHY

A person wishing to do further reading on any topic has to start somewhere. One suggestion is to read about the subject in a good encyclopedia. At the end of the article, there will be suggestions for further reading. Go to one of those sources on the list, and you will discover at the back of the book the bibliography that the author has used. Footnotes at the bottom of the page or end of the chapter also give clues about where to find more information on that specific subject.

Many books have been written about all aspects of the history of the Middle East. The bibliography here lists a small sample of books and articles that will help the teacher and the students understand Middle Eastern history.

Ancient:

Baines, B., L. Lesko, and D. Silverman. *Religion in Ancient Egypt.* Cornell University, 1991.
Bright, J. *A History of Israel.* Louisville: John Knox Press, 1981.
Ceram, C. *Gods, Graves, and Scholars.* New York: Knopf, 1968.
Fox, R. *Alexander the Great.* New York: Dial, 1973.
Glubok, S. *The Discovery of Tutankhamen's Tomb.* New York: Macmillan, 1968.
Grimal, Nicolas. *A History of Ancient Egypt.* Oxford: Blackwell, 1992.
Hallo, W. and W. K. Simpson. *The Ancient and Near East.* New York: Harcourt Brace, 1971.
Keller, W. *The Bible as History.* New York: William Morrow, 1956.
Kramer, S. *The Sumerians: Their History, Culture, and Character.* Chicago: University of Chicago, 1964.
Macqueen, J. *The Hittites and Their Contemporaries.* London: Thames and Hudson, 1986.
Olmstread, A. *History of the Persian Empire.* Chicago, 1948.
Postgate, J. *Early Mesopotamia: Society and Economy at the Dawn of History.* London, 1992.
Roux, G. *Ancient Iraq.* Baltimore, 1980.
Steindorff, G. and K. Seele. *When Egypt Ruled the East.* Chicago: University of Chicago, 1957.
von Soden, W. *The Ancient Orient.* Grand Rapids: Gracewing, 1995.
Wallbank, R. *The Hellenistic World.* Cambridge: Harvard University, 1981.

Medieval and Modern:

Cook, M. *Muhammad.* Oxford University, 1983.
David, R. *Arabs and Israel for Beginners.* Writers and Readers, 1993.
Denny, F. *An Introduction to Islam.* New York: Macmillan, 1994.
Fletcher, R. *Moorish Spain.* University of California Press, 1992.
Friedman, T. *From Beirut to Jerusalem.* New York: Doubleday, 1989.
Goldschmidt, A. Jr. *A Concise History of the Middle East.* Boulder: Westview Press, 1991.
Hitti, P. *History of the Arabs.* New York: St. Martin's Press, 1970.
Hourani, A. *A History of the Arab Peoples.* Cambridge: Belknap Press, 1991.

Kee, H., E. Hanawalt, C. Lindberg, J. Seban, and M. Noll. *Christianity: A Social and Cultural History.* New York: Macmillan, 1991.

Kennedy, H. *The Prophet and the Age of the Caliphates.* London: Longman, 1986.

Lapidus, I. *A History of Islamic Societies.* Cambridge University, 1988.

Lewis, B. *The Shaping of the Modern Middle East.* Oxford University Press, 1994.

Mansfield, P. *A History of the Middle East.* London: Penguin, 1991.

Runciman, S. *Byzantine Civilization.* New York: Barnes and Noble, 1993.

Stewart, D. *Early Islam.* New York: Time-Life, 1967.

Zakaria, R. *Muhammad and the Quran.* London: Penguin, 1991.